"Mark Dever is an able and sure guide to the message of the Bible, which tells us what God wants of us all. The reader of this book is in reliable hands because the author depends not on himself but on the Word of God to answer life's greatest questions. We cannot live lives that please God unless we know what God has said about himself and about us. This book will help you to know God through knowing his Son revealed in his Word."

Thabiti Anyabwile, Senior Pastor,
First Baptist Church of Grand Cayman;
author, *The Faithful Preacher*

"In this fantastic little book, Dever shows us what it means to say that Jesus Christ is the point of the Bible. He offers us a breathtaking, panoramic view of Scripture. Since the message of the Bible is so important, and since Dever has captured that message so succinctly, I'll give this book away again and again—both to Christians eager to get a sense of the whole and to seekers wondering just what the Bible is all about."

Aaron Menikoff, Senior Pastor,
Mount Vernon Bible Church, Sandy Springs, Georgia

"The Bible's size and complexity can overwhelm many new readers. Mark Dever's friendly overview both provides a map to its complexity and downsizes its message to the heart of the matter—what is the passion of God's heart? Keep a bunch of these at your church for giving to anyone unfamiliar with the grand narrative of God's Word."

Matt Schmucker, Executive Director, 9Marks; elder,
Capitol Hill Baptist Church, Washington DC

"Pastor Mark Dever has provided a most unusual book. Instead of teaching his people the usual lessons from the Bible, Dever has taught his people about the Bible so that they can read it effectively for themselves, which is a great idea."

Paige Patterson, President,
Southwestern Baptist Theological Seminary

WHAT DOES GOD
WANT OF US
ANYWAY?

Chris Starr

219) 588- 4656

Other 9Marks books published by Crossway:

WHAT DOES GOD WANT OF US ANYWAY?

A QUICK OVERVIEW OF THE WHOLE BIBLE

MARK DEVER

CROSSWAY

WHEATON, ILLINOIS

What Does God Want of Us Anyway? An Overview of the Whole Bible
Copyright © 2010 by Mark Dever
Published by Crossway Books
      a publishing ministry of Good News Publishers
      1300 Crescent Street
      Wheaton, Illinois 60187

Part 1 and Part 2 originally published in *The Message of the Old Testament: Promises Made* by Mark Dever (Crossway, 2006). Parts 1 and 2 were originally preached each as one sermon on January 9, 2000, and September 1, 1996, respectively, at Capitol Hill Baptist Church in Washington DC.

Part 3 originally published in *The Message of the New Testament: Promises Kept* by Mark Dever (Crossway, 2005). Part 3 was originally preached as one sermon on September 8, 1996, at Capitol Baptist Church in Washington DC.

Cover design: Studio Gearbox
First printing 2010
Printed in the United States of America

Hardcover ISBN:	978-1-4335-1415-9
PDF ISBN:	978-1-4335-1416-6
Mobipocket ISBN:	978-1-4335-1417-3
EPub ISBN:	978-1-4335-2400-4

Library of Congress Cataloging-in-Publication Data
Dever, Mark.
    What does God want of us anyway? : a quick overview of the whole Bible / Mark E. Dever.
       p. cm.
    Parts 1 and 2 originally published in The message of the Old Testament : promises made, 2006. Part 3 originally published in The message of the New Testament : promises kept, 2005.
    ISBN 978-1-4335-1415-9 (hc)—ISBN 978-1-4335-1416-6 (pbk.)—ISBN 978-1-4335-2400-4 (ebk) 1. Bible—Theology. 2. Bible—Criticism, interpretation, etc. 3. Bible—Introductions. 4. Baptists—Sermons. 5. Sermons, American—21st century. I. Title.

BS543.D48   2010
220.6'1—dc22

                                  2009039053

| LB | | 21 | 20 | 19 | 18 | 17 | 16 | 15 | 14 | 13 | 12 | 11 | 10 |
| 14 | 13 | 12 | 11 | 10 | 9 | 8 | 7 | 6 | 5 | 4 | 3 | 2 | 1 |

To
Annie and Nathan

CONTENTS

THE BIG PICTURE

Have you heard of the *Above* series of large coffee-table photography books? There is *Above Washington* and *Above London* and *Above Europe* and many others. I enjoy the series because of the sweeping panoramas it provides. The plans of the original city planners, hidden when walking down the streets with building tops high overhead, suddenly become visible as the pictures let us rise up and look down on the whole. The aerial photographs provide a sense of perspective and interrelatedness, and we see what the planners envisioned in their minds and blueprints.

Clearly, the sense of the whole is important for understanding and for planning. Some people suggest the ecology movement did not begin until the first pictures of the whole earth, taken from space, were published around 1970. Wasn't it on the cover of the old *Whole Earth Catalog*? Seeing a photograph of the earth, I think, jelled our understanding of the world as a whole and galvanized certain individuals to action. In the same way, we want, in the three studies that follow, to pull up and get an "above the Bible" or "whole Bible" view all at once.

Or we might consider the concept of time-lapse photography. In time-lapse photography, the photographer positions the camera to take a shot of the same location multiple times over the course of a day. That allows him to see the changes that occur in one place over a long period of time in just a few moments of flipping through pictures. Reading through the Bible has the same effect. The Bible is, of course, much briefer than what it records. I know it would take you a long time to read it, but it would take you much less time to read it than it took to write it; and it took less time to write it than it took for the events to happen. So the text of Scripture itself is already like a time-lapsed series of photographs. And we want, in the course of the three studies that follow, to flip through an even more condensed series of pictures that present the message of the whole.

The three studies that you can see on the contents page—The Message of the Whole Bible, The Message of the Old Testament, and The Message of the New Testament—began their life as three sermons that I preached to my church, Capitol Hill Baptist Church. Then, several years later, we edited them to read more like chapters in a book and published them together with my "overview sermons" on every book of the Bible. The first two messages appeared in my book *The Message of the Old Testament: Promises Made* (Crossway, 2006), while the third appeared in the companion volume *The Message of the New Testament: Promises Kept* (Crossway, 2005).

Now, Crossway has seen fit to publish just the three studies in one volume, which I pray you find useful.

Since they began as sermons preached at different times, you will find some overlap between them. Still, my hope is that you will find that each presents the burden of the material. God gives life through his Word. He created the world through his Word, and he recreates his people through his Word (Gen. 1:3–4; Ezek. 37:1–10; Rom. 10:14–17; 2 Cor. 4:1–6). Therefore, good preaching is nothing more or less than speaking the burden of God's Word, relying on the Spirit to impress this message into the hearts of sinners. Whether the text you choose to teach is one verse or one Testament, good preaching aims to communicate the burden of that text. What's the burden of the whole Bible? I try to answer that question in The Message of the Whole Bible. What's the burden of the Old Testament? Again, I try to explain that in The Message of the Old Testament. And then I try to do the same in the study on the New Testament.

It's been an immeasurably rich experience for me to try to gaze upon what God has for his people in each Testament as well as the whole Bible. Hopefully, these studies will encourage you to do the same. And where I fail to do Scriptures justice, maybe you will be inspired to do a better job!

Before we continue, let me mention several good resources for helping you understand the Bible further. First, J. I. Packer's *God Has Spoken* will help you understand why you should study and read the Bible as a Christian.[1] Second, whether you are a Christian or a non-Christian, Chris Wright has written a great little book called *User's Guide to the Bible* that will help you know what the Bible contains.[2] It has pictures

---

[1]J. I. Packer, *God Has Spoken* (Downers Grove, IL: InterVarsity, 1979).
[2]Chris Wright, *User's Guide to the Bible* (Belleville, MI: Lion, 1984).

and timelines and bright colors, and it is so very thin! It is a wonderful resource. Finally, Graeme Goldsworthy's little *Gospel and Kingdom*, which comprises the first of three works in his *Goldsworthy Trilogy*, is one of the best treatments of the storyline of the whole Bible.[3] In all of Scripture, Goldsworthy contends, God is bringing his people into his place under his rule.

---

[3]Graeme Goldsworthy, *Gospel and Kingdom: A Christian Interpretation of the Old Testament* (Exeter, UK: Paternoster, 1981); *The Goldsworthy Trilogy* (Exeter, UK: Paternoster, 2000).

THE MESSAGE
OF THE WHOLE BIBLE

ONE GREAT STORY OF PROMISES MADE AND PROMISES KEPT

The Bible has been the subject of numerous and varying opinions.

Many people have not liked it. The great French philosopher Voltaire predicted the Bible would vanish within a hundred years. He said that more than two hundred years ago—in the eighteenth century. His kind of skepticism may have been rare when he lived, but it became more commonplace in the following century. One historian writes, "By the nineteenth century Westerners were already more certain that atoms exist than they were confident of any of the distinctive things the Bible speaks of."[1] By the twentieth century, great sections of the formerly "Christian" parts of the world had fallen into official skepticism about the Bible. *A Dictionary of Foreign Words*, published by the Soviet government about fifty years ago, defined the Bible as, "A collection of different legends, mutually contradictory and written at different

[1]Huston Smith, "Postmodernism and the World's Religion," in Walter Truett Anderson, ed., *The Truth about the Truth: De-Confusing and Re-Constructing the Postmodern World* (New York: Putnam's, 1995), 205.

times and full of historical errors, issued by churches as a 'holy' book."

At the same time, many people have had a very high opinion of the Bible. Ambrose, bishop of Milan in the fourth century, described the Bible beautifully when he said, "As in paradise, God walks in the Holy Scriptures seeking man." Immanuel Kant once stated, "A single line in the Bible has consoled me more than all the books I have ever read." Daniel Webster said of it, "I pity the man who cannot find in it a rich supply of thought and of rules for conduct." Abraham Lincoln called it "the best gift God has given to man." He also claimed, "But for it we could not know right from wrong." Theodore Roosevelt said, "A thorough knowledge of the Bible is worth more than a college education." Certainly one of the most profound understandings of the Bible comes from the great Greek scholar A. T. Robertson, who attested, "Give a man an open Bible, an open mind, a conscience in good working order, and he will have a hard time to keep from being a Baptist."[2]

Some people believe they have great faith in the Bible, yet their sincerity is no guarantee of understanding. King Menelik II, the emperor of Ethiopia a hundred years ago, had great faith in the Bible. Whenever he felt sick, he ripped a few pages from the holy book and ate them! This was his regular practice, and it never did seem to harm him. He was recovering from a stroke in December 1913, when he began to feel particularly sick. He asked an aide to tear out the complete books of 1 and 2 Kings and feed them to him page by page. He died before he could eat both books. Whether

[2]Everett Gill, *A. T. Robertson: A Biography* (New York: Macmillan, 1943), 181.

you like the Bible or not, it has certainly been popular. It is an all-time bestseller. Polls show that Americans generally say they believe the Bible.

Yet the book is probably more purchased than read. Most Americans may not have the gastronomic fervor of King Menelik, which is just fine; but they may also have less knowledge of the Bible than he did. Pollster George Gallup reports:

> Americans revere the Bible, but they don't read it. And because they don't read it, they have become a nation of biblical illiterates. Four Americans in five believe the Bible is the literal or inspired Word of God, and yet only 4 in 10 could tell you that it was Jesus who gave the Sermon on the Mount and fewer than half can name the Four Gospels. . . . The cycle of biblical illiteracy seems likely to continue—today's teenagers know even less about the Bible than do adults. The celebration of Easter . . . is central to the faith, yet 3 teenagers in 10—20 percent of regular churchgoing teens—do not even know why Easter is celebrated. The decline in Bible reading is due in part to the widely held conviction that the Bible is inaccessible and less emphasis on religious training in the churches.[3]

It is exactly such ignorance we hope to help remove with this study. You or I may not be able to learn everything about Christianity in one fell swoop. In fact, I am certain we cannot. But I do hope to bring your attention to the overarching theme of the Bible as well as the basic message of Christianity, or what is called "the gospel."

[3]Cited by Michael S. Horton, "Recovering the Plumb Line," in John H. Armstrong, ed., *The Coming Evangelical Crisis: Current Challenges to the Authority of Scripture and the Gospel* (Chicago: Moody, 1996), 259.

Many people are surprised to hear that the Bible has any sort of overarching theme or story. It is well known as a collection of books. As one Bible scholar put it:

> No less than sixty-six separate books, one of which consists itself of one hundred and fifty separate compositions, immediately stare us in the face. These treatises come from the hands of at least thirty distinct writers, scattered over a period of some fifteen hundred years, and embrace specimens of nearly every kind of writing known among men. Histories, codes of law, ethical maxims, philosophical treatises, discourses, dramas, songs, hymns, epics, biographies, letters both official and personal, vaticinations. . . .
>
> Their writers, too, were of like diverse kinds. The time of their labors stretches from the hoary past of Egypt to and beyond the bright splendor of Rome under Augustus. . . .
>
> We may look, however, on a still greater wonder. Let us once penetrate beneath all this primal diversity and observe the internal character of the volume, and a most striking unity is found to pervade the whole. . . . The parts are so linked together that the absence of any one book would introduce confusion and disorder. The same doctrine is taught from beginning to end. . . . Each book, indeed, adds something in clearness, definition, or even increment, to what the others proclaim.[4]

Clearly, the Bible is made up of many parts. Yet this book is one whole: "utter diversity in origin of these books, and yet utter nicety of combination of one with all."[5] It tells one great story.

[4]B. B. Warfield, "The Divine Origin of the Bible," in *Revelation and Inspiration*, The Works of Benjamin B. Warfield (Grand Rapids, MI: Baker, 1981), 1:436–37.
[5]Ibid., 437.

The storyline that we will follow—and the outline of the next six chapters—is the story of promises made and promises kept. God makes promises to his people in the Old Testament, and he keeps his promises in the New Testament. This message of promises made and promises kept is the most important message in all the world, including for you. Maybe you will "get it" in this study. Or maybe it will get you. As Martin Luther said, "The Bible is alive, it speaks to me; it has feet, it runs after me; it has hands, it lays hold on me." I pray that happens to you.

A PARTICULAR HISTORY

Not everyone who reads the Bible regards it as one whole. Some ignore the Old Testament. Toward the close of the second century, the followers of a man named Marcion rejected the Old Testament, even though the Old Testament was the Bible of Jesus and the apostles. No Christian today says exactly what Marcion said, but the effect is the same: we may mine it for good stories about Joseph, David, or Moses. We look for good examples of bravery or devotion for our children to emulate. But on the whole, we ignore it. Is it just laziness?

If you are a Christian, you surely know of God's wonderful revelation of himself in Christ as recorded in the New Testament. Yet if you ignore the Old Testament, you ignore the basis and foundation of the New. The context for understanding the person and work of Christ is the Old Testament. God's work of creation, humanity's rebellion against him, sin's consequence in death, God's election of a particular people, his revelation of sin through the law, the history of his people, his work among other peoples—I could go on and on—all these form the setting for Christ's coming. Christ came in history at a particular point in the storyline. So the parables taught by

Jesus often refer back to the storyline begun in Genesis. His verbal battles with the Pharisees are rooted in differences over the meaning of the law. And the Epistles build upon the Old Testament again and again. Understanding God's purpose in history, understanding the storyline, requires us to begin at the beginning. If we can better understand the Old Testament, we will have gone a long way toward better understanding the New Testament and, therefore, better understanding Jesus Christ, Christianity, God, and ourselves.

Over this chapter and the next two, we will consider what God teaches us through the Old Testament. First, we will consider a particular history. Second, we will consider God's passion for holiness. Third, we will observe the Old Testament's promise of hope.

In this chapter, we start with a particular history.

The Story

The Old Testament text begins, not surprisingly, on page 1 of your Bible: "In the beginning God created the heavens and the earth" (Gen. 1:1). That is where the storyline of a particular history begins. The Bible is not only a book of wise religious counsel and theological propositions, though it has both. It is a story, a real story set in real history. It is a historical saga—an epic. And the story in the Old Testament is amazing!

In this very first verse, the story begins with the greatest event in world history. You have nothing, and then all of a sudden you have something.

But keep reading; there is more! You have inanimate creation, and then all of a sudden you have life.

You have creatures, and then you have man made in God's image.

You have the garden of Eden, and then you have the fall.

And all this occurs in the first three chapters of the Bible. Some people have called the third chapter of Genesis, where Adam and Eve sin in the garden, the most important chapter for understanding the whole Bible. Cut out Genesis 3, and the rest of the Bible would be meaningless.

After Adam and Eve's sin, Cain kills his brother Abel. Humankind further degenerates for a number of generations. And God finally judges the world with a flood, saving just one righteous man—Noah—and his family.

The generations following Noah fare no better. Humankind rebels at the Tower of Babel; this time God disperses everyone over the face of the earth.

A new beginning is then promised as God shows his faithfulness to another particular person, Abraham, and his family. After a brief period of prosperity, Abraham's descendents, now called Israel, fall into slavery in Egypt.

Then the exodus occurs, in which Moses leads the people out of Egypt. God gives Israel the law. The people enter the Promised Land. They are ruled by a series of judges for a short time. A kingdom is established, with kings David and David's son Solomon representing the pinnacle. Solomon builds the temple, which houses the ark of the covenant and functions as the center of Israel's worship of Yahweh.

Shortly after Solomon's death, the kingdom divides between Israel and Judah—the northern and southern kingdoms. Idolatry grows in Israel until the Assyrians destroy the northern kingdom. Judah then deteriorates until it is destroyed by

Babylon. Survivors are carried off to exile in Babylon, where they remain for seventy years.

A remnant then returns to Jerusalem and rebuilds the temple, yet Israel never regains the glory it knew under David and Solomon. And that is the whole history of the Old Testament!

The Books

If you turn to the table of contents in your Bible, you can see that this storyline is not recounted in just one book but in thirty-nine smaller books. These books, which together make up the Old Testament, are quite different from one another. Genesis through Deuteronomy, the first five books, is called the Pentateuch or the five books of the Law. Following these five are twelve books called the Histories—Joshua through Esther. Taken together, these seventeen books chronicle the narrative from creation to the exiles' return, and they conclude about four hundred years before Christ. All seventeen books, one after the other, are fairly chronological.

The five books that follow the historical narrative books in your table of contents—Job, Psalms, Proverbs, Ecclesiastes, and Song of Solomon—focus on some of the more personal experiences of the people of God. These books are largely collections taken from throughout this Old Testament period of wisdom literature, devotional poems, and ceremonial literature from the temple.

Following Song of Solomon, you will see in the table of contents a series of seventeen books, beginning with Isaiah and ending with Malachi, the last book of the Old Testament. These are the Prophets. If the first seventeen books follow

Israel's history, and the middle group describes individual experiences within that history, this last group provides God's own commentary on the history. The books of prophecy are, as it were, God's authoritative editorials.

The Revelation

So the Old Testament as a whole provides one very clear and concrete revelation of God to his people, given through a variety of authors and genres over a long stretch of time. And through that revelation it gives us a particular history.

What a tremendous way God has chosen to reveal himself to us! If you have ever been in a position to hire someone, you know what it is like to get a one-page résumé that attempts to sum up an individual. And you know how unsatisfying a one-page summary is for knowing an individual and making an important decision. Meeting and interacting with someone in person is much more revealing. Well, in the Old Testament, God provides us far more than a flat résumé. He gives us an account of how he worked with his people over the ages. We see how he treated them. We see how they responded to him. We see what he is like. And that brings us to the second thing for us to notice about the Old Testament if we want to understand the message of the Bible, which we turn to in the next chapter.

CHAPTER THREE

A PASSION FOR HOLINESS

The Old Testament presents us not only with the particular history of Israel; it introduces us to God's passion for holiness. The question this raises is, what does this mean for an unholy people?

A lot of people associate the Old Testament with an angry God. They even think of this Old Testament God as unjust. But nothing could be further from the truth. He's a God of love who makes covenants. When God becomes angry in the Old Testament, you can be sure it is not whimsical tyranny. He is committed to his own holy and glorious character, and he is committed to his covenant with his people. Sin, the culprit that stirs up God's anger, robs God of glory and breaks his covenant with his people.[1]

Covenant

What is meant by this language of "covenant"? Christians refer to a "covenant" when they gather at the Lord's Supper and recall Jesus' words, "This cup is the new covenant in

[1] Prov. 15:29; Isa. 59:2; Hab. 1:13; also Col. 1:21; Heb. 10:27.

my blood" (Luke 22:20). Jesus' language of covenant is not cold or legal, as some might think; he takes it from the Old Testament language for relationship-making. A covenant is a relational commitment of trust, love, and care, and God makes a number of covenants with his people in the Old Testament—with Abraham, Moses, and others. God's passion for holiness becomes most evident when his people break the terms of their covenantal relationship with him, terms that are defined by the Mosaic Law and that accord with his own holy character. So we can define sin as law breaking, but we also know that law breaking means covenant breaking, relationship breaking, and—at the deepest level—"God's holiness defying." So does the Old Testament present us with an angry God? Yes, but it is a God who is angry exactly because he is not indifferent to sin and the incredible pain and suffering it causes.

Like the New Testament, the Old Testament teaches that every man and woman is a sinner, and that no one can deal with this by himself or herself.[2] Sin requires some kind of reparation. But how can reparation occur? God is holy, and justice can be restored only, it would seem, when God justly condemns the person who has wickedly broken his law (the terms of his covenant with Moses). So the sinner must be condemned! Or—and here is our only hope—some type of atonement must be made.

Atonement

What is atonement? Our English word *atonement*, Anglo-Saxon in origin, is a great picture of what the word means—

---

[2] 1 Kings 8:46; Ps. 14:3; Prov. 20:9; Eccles. 7:20; also Mark 10:18; Rom. 3:23.

at-one-ment. An offering of atonement enables two warring parties to be at one, or reconciled. The people of Israel were not the only people in the ancient Near Eastern world who knew they needed atonement before God; the idea of placating a deity was common, yet only the Old Testament places the idea of atonement within the context of a genuine covenantal relationship between God and man.

Atonement in the Old Testament is unique in another way. As in many cultures, it is linked with sacrifice. But in the Bible, a sacrifice of atonement does not depend on human initiative, such as some pitiful attempt to propitiate a volcano god by dropping a beloved object into the fire. In the Old Testament, the living God speaks, and he tells his people how to approach him. He takes the initiative in providing the way of reconciliation.

Sacrifice

Sacrifice is not the only image the Old Testament uses to describe atonement,[3] but it does play a central role from the beginning. Immediately after the fall, Cain and Abel offer sacrifices (Gen. 4:3–4). Before leaving Egypt, the Israelites are commanded to slaughter a Passover lamb without defect and paint its blood on the doors of their houses (Exodus 12). The lamb's blood causes the Spirit of God to pass over a house, sparing the life of a family's firstborn (who represents the whole family) from God's just punishment of sin. In all of this, God very clearly is the object of the sacrificial event. Sacrifices

[3]For instance, Isaiah uses the image of a hot coal that purges unclean lips (Isa. 6:6–7); Hosea describes the purchase of an offender (Hos. 3:2–3); Zechariah refers to the removing of filthy clothes (Zech. 3:4).

are done to satisfy him and his just requirements. So God says to Moses, "When I see the blood . . ." (Ex. 12:13).

The book of Leviticus played a large role in teaching the Israelite people that their relationship with God needed to be restored through a sacrifice. Every sacrifice was to be voluntary, costly, accompanied by a confession of sin, and according to God's prescriptions. The life of the animal victim, symbolized by its blood, was given in exchange for the life of the guilty human worshiper. What does some animal have to do with an individual's guilt? In one sense, nothing. In fact, the animal was supposed to be unblemished.[4] Yet atonement had to be made through blood.[5] God tells the people that "the life of a creature is in the blood, and I have given it to you to make atonement for yourselves on the altar; it is the blood that makes atonement for one's life" (Lev. 17:11). God used the sacrificial act to implant in his people's minds the image of an innocent life being given in exchange for guilty lives. The shed blood plainly revealed that sin causes death. Sin is costly. Salvation and forgiveness are costly. Now, I know the whole idea of sacrifices and all that blood is unpopular—to say the least!—among many people today. Still, this is how the Old Testament shows God's holiness and his wrath against sin. Unlike other ancient sacrifices, biblical sacrifices were not made by the grateful so much as by the guilty; they were not made by the ignorant so much as by the instructed.

The design of the Old Testament temple was also used to teach the people that their sin separated them from God. In the back of your Bible you might find a diagram of the

[4]E.g., Lev. 1:3, 10; 3:1, 6; 4:3, 23, 28.
[5]E.g., Gen. 9:5; Lev. 1:4; 4:4; 14:51; 16:21.

temple that shows that it was designed as a series of concentric squares and rectangles. The worshipers on the outside were separated from God in the innermost square, called the Most Holy Place. The temple's design physically demonstrated that sin hinders access to God. It was a visual picture of how sin separates humans from their Creator. Aside from the sacrifices that occurred throughout the year in the outer court, the high priest entered the Most Holy Place once a year to offer a sacrifice for all the people (Leviticus 16). This was the Day of Atonement.

Yet the mere fact that the sacrifices had to be repeated annually showed that the sacrifices, in and of themselves, were never the point.[6] Their repetition showed instead that the people were in a state of sin, and that no perfect and complete sacrifice could take away sin entirely. Sacrifices were most efficacious, ironically, when they were made with the understanding that they were not efficacious and that only God's grace saves. But notice the problem here. If the sacrifices were not finally effective for the removing of sin, how could God's grace justly save?

A Riddle

Here we come to the riddle of the Old Testament. In Exodus 34, God refers to himself by saying, "The LORD, the LORD, the compassionate and gracious God, slow to anger, abounding in love and faithfulness, maintaining love to thousands, and forgiving wickedness, rebellion and sin. Yet he does not leave the guilty unpunished" (vv. 6–7). Now, how can that

---

[6]As you can tell if you read Jeremiah's denunciations of them in Jeremiah 7.

be? How can God forgive "wickedness, rebellion and sin" and yet "not leave the guilty unpunished"?

The good news is, the God of the Old Testament has a passion for holiness, but he also promises hope. And that brings us to the last thing we need to understand about the Old Testament and the God it reveals.

CHAPTER FOUR

A PROMISE OF HOPE

The Old Testament does not portray God as an uncaring dispenser of grim condemnation. Yes, he is holy, just, and unwavering in his commitment to punish sin, as he is in the New Testament. But the God of the Old Testament is also a God of love who offers a promise of hope, even toward his enemies. He is the "compassionate and gracious God, slow to anger, abounding in love and faithfulness" (Ex. 34:6). Love is not a uniquely Christian thing; it is a biblical thing.

Love

The Old Testament enjoins love in many places. For instance, what Jesus will eventually call the greatest command is first given to Israel: "Love the LORD your God with all your heart and with all your soul and with all your strength" (Deut. 6:5). The second command that follows from the first comes from the Old Testament as well: "Love him [a foreigner living among you] as yourself" (Lev. 19:34).

And the pattern for how Israel should love is how God himself loves: "He defends the cause of the fatherless and the widow, and loves the alien, giving him food and clothing. And you are to love those who are aliens, for you yourselves were aliens in Egypt" (Deut. 10:18–19).

Since God loves his enemies, his people must do the same. Proverbs 24 commands, "Do not gloat when your enemy falls; when he stumbles, do not let your heart rejoice" (v. 17).

And Proverbs 25 teaches, "If your enemy is hungry, give him food to eat; if he is thirsty, give him water to drink" (v. 21).

The God of the Old Testament is a God of love.

Forbearance

When we consider the whole sweep of Old Testament history and observe God's patience toward those who have declared themselves his enemies through disobedience, we see a God of unspeakable love and forbearance. He did not have to let human history continue after the fall in the garden. He did not have to persevere with the wayward nation of Israel. Yet we watch his grace, love, mercy, and patience on an epic scale—stretched out across the history of a people.

It almost looks as if God planned to use history to reveal his glory to his people. And in fact, he did.

Hope

Understanding the Old Testament, as I said, requires understanding its promise of hope. What hope? We have talked plenty about God's commitment to holiness and the failure of his people to live up to the requirements of holiness. And we have considered God's promise to punish the wicked (in Exodus 34). So what hope could sinners have?

   Their hope was not in their history. The history of the Old Testament proved them (and us) to be moral and spiritual failures.

   Nor was their hope finally in the sacrificial system. As the psalmist said, "Sacrifice and offering you did not desire,"[1] at least not without something even more basic.

   How then could the hope held out in Exodus 34:6–7 be true? How could God "forgive wickedness" and still "not leave the guilty unpunished"?

   If the answer was not in the Old Testament people themselves or in their own history, it was in God and his promise, particularly in God's promised person. As we have seen, blood must be shed in order to assuage the righteous wrath of God against sin. Justice demands that sin be paid for either by the guilty party himself or herself or by an innocent substitute who bears the suffering and death on behalf of the guilty party. Furthermore, the punishment of a substitute requires some sort of relation between the guilty one and the one being offered as the sacrifice. But where would a perfect substitute be found?

A Messiah

Sources from the first century suggest that messianic hope and expectation were prominent at the time of Jesus' birth. People

---

[1]Ps. 40:6. The psalmist, among other Old Testament writers, seemed to share the insight of the New Testament writer to the Hebrews, who wrote, "The law . . . can never, by the same sacrifices repeated endlessly year after year, make perfect those who draw near to worship. If it could, would they not have stopped being offered? For the worshipers would have been cleansed once for all, and would no longer have felt guilty for their sins. But those sacrifices are an annual reminder of sins, because it is impossible for the blood of bulls and goats to take away sins" (Heb. 10:1–4).

did not wonder if the Messiah would come. They took it for granted that their only hope lay with a specially anointed one of God—the Messiah. Why? The Old Testament is filled with the promise of a coming person. God's people waited for the prophet God promised to Moses (Deut. 18:15–19). They waited for the king and, perhaps, the suffering servant (Isa. 9:6; 11:1–5; 53). They waited for the son of man coming on the clouds seen by Daniel (Dan. 7:13).

These promises point toward the answer to the Old Testament riddle. And these promises are the hope of the Old Testament. More than anything else, in fact, the Old Testament teaches us that these promises offer us our only hope.

The fulfillment of these hopes, however, would not come in the Old Testament, but in the new, which we turn to now.

CHAPTER FIVE

THE PROMISED REDEEMER: CHRIST

I wonder what you have your hopes set on. This is a crucial question for both you and me to answer. Many, even most, of our problems come from attaching our hopes to things that were not made to bear them—things that will sink like stones in water and pull us down with them. Some things even hold out great promise in the beginning but eventually prove to be passing fancies, or worse. In this old world, it's not only in politics where promises made are *not* necessarily promises kept.

So we must turn to God. He made us and knows us. He knows where our hopes should be placed. He has set before us in the Old Testament the very promises upon which we should set our hope. And we look to the New Testament to find the fulfillment of those promises.

The nation of Israel had waxed and waned for almost two millennia until their hopes almost vanished. Even after their release from Babylonian exile, only several hundred years passed before another alien invader crushed them—the mighty Roman Empire. Feelings of disappointment verged on despair. What about all their old hopes? Would their deliverer never come? Would fellowship with God never be restored? Would the world never be put right? God had promised his people all these things.

And God delivered on his promises. The New Testament is the story of how all the promises God made in the Old Testament, God kept.

We'll consider God's work of fulfillment in this chapter and the next two. First we will look at Christ, then at God's covenant people, and finally at the renewal of all creation. You might be helped by thinking of these three themes as three concentric circles. We begin with the heart of the matter and move outward. In all of this, we find that God has penetrated human history and has worked for his own purposes.

A Promised Deliverer

First, would Israel's deliverer ever come? The New Testament answers this Old Testament promise with a resounding yes! In fact, the one who fulfills this promise is the very center of the New Testament: Jesus Christ.

The New Testament teaches that before history began God planned to send Christ. Adam and Eve rebelled against God's rightful rule in the garden, and God's people rebelled continuously over millennia. Yet God's plan remained in place through everything. An anointed deliverer would come—a Messiah (Hebrew) or a Christ (Greek). And he would come from a tattered remnant of Israel living amid Roman occupation.

Jesus in the Gospels and Acts

The collection of twenty-seven books that comprise the New Testament begins by directly addressing this promise with four accounts of the life of the Messiah. The four documentaries of Matthew, Mark, Luke, and John all argue that Jesus of Nazareth is the Messiah. He is the promised one for whom God's people have been waiting. Where Adam and Israel failed, Jesus was faithful. As did his predecessors, he faced Satan's temptations. Yet he survived them without sin. He is the prophet promised by Moses, the king prefigured by David, and the divine son of man promised by Daniel. In fact, Jesus is the very Word of God made flesh (John 1:1, 14).

Following these first four, the next book in the New Testament, Acts, shows how Jesus continues to be active in the world as his church expands to all nations. Acts begins with Jesus' ascending to heaven and then giving out his Spirit at Pentecost. Over the ensuing chapters, his Spirit establishes the church as God's new society and empowers it to grow and to do Christ's work. The book concludes with Paul's imprisonment in Rome.

We see the fulfillment of God's Old Testament promises to his people frequently in the book of Acts (e.g., 15:13–18), and this pattern is typical of the whole New Testament. Jesus is the new Adam (1 Cor. 15:45–47). Jesus is the righteous one (Acts 3:14; 1 Pet. 3:18; 1 John 2:1). Jesus is greater than Moses (John 1:17; 5:45–46; Heb. 3:1–6) and greater than David (Matt. 22:41–45; Acts 2:29–36). Abraham, Jesus said, rejoiced to see his day (John 8:56–58). According to the New Testament, promises made in the Old Testament are promises kept in Jesus.

The Point of the Bible

Indeed, Jesus Christ is the point of the Bible. It is all about him. If you wanted to sum up the Bible in one word, you could do so by pointing to Christ. The Old Testament makes promises about Christ, and the New Testament keeps promises in Christ.

We read the Bible because we love Christ, and we want to know more about his love for us. John Stott writes, "A man who loves his wife will love her letters and her photographs because they speak to him of her. So if we love the Lord Jesus we shall love the Bible because it speaks to us of him. The husband is not so stupid as to prefer his wife's letters to her voice, or her photographs to herself. He simply loves them because of her. So, too, we love the Bible because of Christ. It is his portrait. It is his love-letter."[1] There are cold religious legalists who fight for the Bible but who do not love the Lord described in its pages. The Bible shows us Christ so that we can look to him as the focus of our hopes and the center of our satisfaction.

In him we find all the answers we need about God and his call on our lives. Christ is the promised deliverer not just for God's Old Testament people but for you and me as well.

[1] John Stott, *Fundamentalism and Evangelism* (Grand Rapids, MI: Eerdmans, 1959), 41.

CHAPTER SIX

THE PROMISED RELATIONSHIP: A NEW-COVENANT PEOPLE

The work and person of Jesus Christ are at the very center of the New Testament, as we considered in the last chapter. When we move one step outward to our second concentric circle for understanding the New Testament, we find Christ's people: Christ came for a people!

Because of sin, mankind, though created in the image of God, lost the ability to perfectly image God. Christ came and displayed that image once more. But not only that! He came to make a people for God, a special covenant people particularly called to reflect God's image to all creation. We have seen that the "covenant" language in the Bible is not cold, legal language, but relational language. We have also seen that Jesus Christ uses this sort of language of Christians when he offers us the "new covenant in my blood"—words we recall when we partake of the Lord's Supper. This new covenant signifies the new relationship that we Christians, God's people, have with God.

Christ as a Mediator for His People

How did Christ accomplish this? At one point, Jesus says to his followers, "Destroy this temple, and I will raise it again in three days" (John 2:19). He was standing in the temple at the time, but he did not mean the building; he meant himself. In the New Testament, Jesus himself is the new temple. He is the new meeting place for God and his people. He is the mediator.

You see, Christ came not only to fulfill the Old Testament hope for Messiah as prophet and king; he came to fulfill the hope for a priest. Jesus our mediating priest grants us a new relationship with God by solving the riddle of the Old Testament which we saw at the close of chapter 4: how can the Lord "forgive wickedness" and yet "not leave the guilty unpunished"? When Jesus was nailed to the cross, the guilt of all who would ever repent and put their trust in him was punished. He received that punishment! He stood in for the guilty, so that the guilty might be forgiven. After his resurrection, Jesus used the Old Testament to teach these lessons:

> Beginning with Moses and all the Prophets, he explained to them what was said in all the Scriptures concerning himself. . . .
>
> Then he opened their minds so they could understand the Scriptures. He told them, "This is what is written: The Christ will suffer and rise from the dead on the third day, and repentance and forgiveness of sins will be preached in his name to all nations, beginning at Jerusalem." (Luke 24:27, 45–47)

Christ's suffering provides a way for us his people to be forgiven, which is exactly what the Lord had promised through the prophet Isaiah:

Surely he took up our infirmities
    and carried our sorrows,
yet we considered him stricken by God,
    smitten by him, and afflicted.
But he was pierced for our transgressions,
    he was crushed for our iniquities;
the punishment that brought us peace was upon him,
    and by his wounds we are healed.
We all, like sheep, have gone astray,
    each of us has turned to his own way;
and the LORD has laid on him the iniquity of us all. (Isa.
    53:4–6)

This is what Christ did! He was pierced. He was crushed. And he had our iniquities laid upon him. His own body provides the priestly sacrifice we need to stand in between God and us so that we might be God's own people. As Jesus taught his disciples, "the Son of Man did not come to be served, but to serve, and to give his life as a ransom for many" (Mark 10:45; cf. Gal. 4:4–5; Philippians 2).

Christ as Substitute for His People

In giving himself, Christ combined an amazing strength and humility. One of the best portrayals of this occurs in Revelation 5. The apostle John is told to look and see the Lion of the tribe of Judah. He turns to see the Lion, but what does he behold? A Lamb. The message is not that there are two gods; the message is that the Lion is the Lamb. The Lion of

Judah has become the Lamb slain for our sins. This is the story of our great God. He has become our sacrificial lamb—our substitute. And by acting as our substitute, he has purchased us, his church, with his own blood (Acts 20:28).

So Christ is the answer to the Old Testament's riddle. And in Christ, the people are made holy. The very thing that God wanted of his people in the Old Testament, that he planned toward, that they never achieved on their own, God now has through Christ: a remnant, a nation, a people to praise him with lips and lives of holiness. He has a new-covenant people who are genuinely holy in Christ.

The Scriptures for Our Salvation and Holiness

When we open the New Testament, we find throughout its pages this all-important emphasis on salvation from sin to holiness. Paul tells the Ephesian Christians they have been saved (Eph. 2:8–9). He tells the Corinthian Christians they are being saved (1 Cor. 1:18). And he tells the Christians in Rome they shall be saved (Rom. 5:9). Christians are already counted as holy in Christ; we are being made holy even now; and someday, thanks to God, we will be holy in ourselves. The work of the kingdom of God has begun in us, and we look forward to its completion.

The New Testament paints the contrast between the world and the kingdom of God starkly. The world is marked by unbelief; the kingdom of God is marked by faith. The world is characterized by bondage and darkness; the covenant people of God enjoy freedom and light. The world knows only death; those belonging to the kingdom are promised eternal life. Hate and fear typify the first; love typifies the second. Apart from the covenant in Christ, our lives are marked by lawlessness. In Christ, we abide in God. The Scriptures have been given to the people of God so that they will perceive these contrasts, discover where salvation is found, and know what God's judgment will entail. So our own church's statement of faith (taken from the 1833 New Hampshire Confession) begins with the words:

> Of The Scriptures: We believe that the Holy Bible was written by men divinely inspired, and is a perfect treasure of heavenly instruction; that it has God for its author, salvation for its end, and truth without any mixture of error for its matter; that it reveals the principles by which God will judge us; and therefore is, and shall remain to the end of the world, the true centre of Christian union, and the supreme standard by which all human conduct, creeds, and opinions should be tried.

Books of the New Testament

Following after the Gospels, which focus on the identity of Jesus Christ, the rest of the New Testament helps define and fill out what it means for us to be the special covenant people of Christ. If you look back to the table of contents for the New Testament, you see the four Gospels. Then you see the book of Acts, which is really the transition from these Gospels to the books about living as God's people. In Acts, the gospel expands outward from Jerusalem, to Judea, to Samaria, and, beginning with the three missionary journeys of Paul, to the ends of the world. After Acts you see a number of books that are letters, and these letters describe what it means to live as God's specially covenanted people.

Paul wrote the first thirteen of these letters. Originally a noted rabbi of the stricter sort of Jews, Paul was remarkably converted by God as he was traveling, in his words, to persecute some Christians "to their death" (Acts 22:4).

Following Paul's letters are eight more, written by James, Peter, John, Jude, and one unknown author (Hebrews). As we read through all of these letters, we find that the promises made by God in the Old Testament have been kept in God's new-covenant people. You see, God has desired to show himself not merely in Christ but in a community of people who live and love one another in a manner that displays God's character to the world. If we are Christians, that is happening this very day in our churches!

Thy Kingdom Come

As Christians, we often pray, "Thy kingdom come. Thy will be done in earth, as it is in heaven" (Matt. 6:10 KJV). Have you ever wondered what that means? Some people limit their hopes to those things they can achieve in their own strength. But Christianity has never been like that. As Christians, we have always put our hope in something that goes beyond what we can bring about by our own power. Peter writes in his second letter, "We are looking forward to a new heaven and a new earth, the home of righteousness" (2 Pet. 3:13). This kingdom come, this new heaven and new earth, this home of righteousness, points us to the fulfillment of our final and first hope: the whole world being put right. This is the third movement of God's plan in the New Testament as it extends from Christ to his covenant people to the outermost circle—his whole creation. Let's turn there now.

CHAPTER SEVEN

THE PROMISED RENEWAL: A NEW CREATION

What is the point of history? Why do life and the universe and you and I exist at all? All history and all creation exist ultimately for God's glory. This is what we find at the conclusion of the New Testament. In the last book of the Bible, Revelation, written by the apostle John, all creation is taken up into God's glory.

The Book of Revelation

I know the book of Revelation is sometimes the subject of sensationalistic documentaries with ominous music. But Revelation is actually a book of wonderful hope and encouragement for God's people. It presents the consummation of our salvation. We are finally in God's place, under his rule, and in a perfectly right relationship to him. The heavens and the earth are re-created, and the struggling church militant becomes the resting church triumphant (see Rev. 21:1–4; 21:22–22:5).

Some people get to Revelation and say, "This is just idealistic Greek Platonism." Or, "This is just another world-denying

gnosticism, as if only the invisible matters." But that is not
what John presents us at all. In Revelation, creation is re-
finished, refurbished, and re-presented in a new heaven and
a new earth, all of which tends toward the great end of the
Bible and world history—the glory of God himself. That is
no Platonism or gnosticism! As Christians, we do not merely
believe in an eternal soul that ascends and lives with God in
the clouds. We believe in a doctrine that was offensive to the
ancient Greeks: the resurrection of the body.

In a manner beyond our comprehension, God will one day
reconstitute these presently rotting bodies of ours. Jesus' own
resurrection was only the "firstfruits." It was the beginning of
the great harvest to follow (1 Cor. 15:20). And his remaking of
our bodies is a picture of what he will do with all creation.

Dwelling with God

The holiness of God's people will finally be complete, and
we will dwell together with him. Really, Revelation presents
the garden of Eden restored, only better. Now it is a heavenly
and perfect city, a city that works not because the sewers are
good and the taxes are low but because God abides with his
people. John describes the measurements of this heavenly city
as a great cube. Any Christian who knows the Old Testament
knows that John's vision harks back to the Most Holy Place.
This special place within Israel's temple was itself a perfect
cube and the most manifest location of God's presence on
earth. Now, in this cube-shaped heavenly city, God's full,
unmediated presence is given to all his people. The whole
world becomes the temple. John writes:

> And I heard a loud voice from the throne saying, "Now the dwelling of God is with men, and he will live with them. They will be his people, and God himself will be with them and be their God. He will wipe every tear from their eyes. There will be no more death or mourning or crying or pain, for the old order of things has passed away." (Rev. 21:3–4)

Since we know what this world is all about, we Christians have great news to offer.

The Purpose of Life

I remember sitting cross-legged one day in an undergraduate philosophy class at Duke University in a room with purple shag carpet on the floor, walls, and ceiling, lit by one dangling lightbulb (I am dating myself quite clearly). The professor began the hour by asking the question, "What's the purpose of life?" Well, nobody would say anything, because these days answering that kind of question sounds prideful. But I was a young Christian, and the silence was killing me. I remember thinking to myself that here were all these people made in the image of God, and I was not saying anything. So I finally blurted out, "The purpose of life is to glorify God and to enjoy him forever!"

Christian friend, that is the purpose of life! We are not clueless about that fact. You may not know why you are in the job you are in. You may not know why you have the disease that you have. You may not know a lot of very significant things. But right now, you know the most significant thing in all the world: the purpose of life is to know God so that you may glorify him and enjoy him forever.

A Time of Waiting and Hope

Presently, we live in a time of waiting, and for that reason the book of Revelation appropriately concludes the New Testament. It was written by an old man who had been left alone and deserted in exile. Everything this world values had been taken from him, and he was utterly desperate. Still, he was full of hope!

And that is Christianity. We are to live filled with such hope. God has promised that the earth will be filled with the knowledge of his glory, and he will keep this promise in his new creation. Every promise made by God will be kept by God.

BELIEVING GOD'S PROMISES

We all know that some disappointments have their uses. The ruins of cherished plans are often the first steps to the true good that God has in store for us. The apostle Paul learned this when he asked God to remove the thorn in his flesh (2 Cor. 12:7–9). God, in his great and strange mercy, said no. Nationalistic Israelites also learned this in how they were waiting for the Messiah. God had something better in his plans than the immediate political supremacy of Israel over her enemies.

And that is true in your life and mine. Neither you nor I have a life perfectly attuned to the will, desires, and hopes of God. So we will inevitably face disappointment. We will watch the things we fix our hopes upon sink like stones in water.

Yet it is God's grace to us that they do. As strange as it may seem, if we really believe the Bible, we must learn to trust that he knows what he is doing, and that his plans for us are better than whatever we have planned for ourselves. So often we cling with all our might to what we have in this world. But God has something even better prepared for his children.

If you are a child of God through new birth in Christ, the conclusion God has in mind for you is unimaginably good! As John writes in one of his letters, "Dear friends, now we are children of God, and what we will be has not yet been made known. But we know that when he appears, we shall be like him, for we shall see him as he is" (1 John 3:2). Paul, also, dissolves into doxology when he thinks of what God has done and will do: "Oh, the depth of the riches of the wisdom and knowledge of God! How unsearchable his judgments, and his paths beyond tracing out!" (Rom. 11:33).

An Illustration of Trust

Of course, our minds are not always fixed on such lofty things. We are not always sitting in church or reading sermons about the whole Bible. Very often, our lives are consumed with other hopes, and we look for contentment amid smaller things.

William Wilberforce was such a man. He thought he possessed everything a man could want. He was born into an old family in Yorkshire, England, in 1759. He grew up in great privilege, was given to ease, and had a wonderful wit. He did well in his undergraduate studies at Cambridge University, where he also befriended William Pitt, who very soon became the prime minister of England. Almost immediately upon graduating from Cambridge in 1781, Wilberforce was elected to Parliament. He was very fashionable and quickly became prominent in London because of his close friendships with many important society and political leaders. He soon defined the "in" crowd and even in his early twenties held a position of considerable power and eminence.

In the winter of 1784–1785, Wilberforce toured the south of France with several friends, among them Isaac Milner. On the trip, Wilberforce made frequent jibes at what he thought was the overheated piety of evangelical Christians. Unbeknownst to the witty Wilberforce, his traveling companion Milner was such a Christian. At one point, Wilberforce referred to one prominent evangelical leader by saying he was a good man but that he "carried things a bit too far." Milner, who had not yet remonstrated his young friend, responded, "Not a bit too far." He suggested that carefully perusing the whole New Testament might cause Wilberforce to form a different estimate of this man. Wilberforce, a little surprised at his friend's forwardness, said he would. And he did!

Over the next few weeks on that trip, God used the Bible to make William Wilberforce a new man. As he later told it, the Bible's message about God and man, sin and Christ's sacrifice, the forgiveness and new birth that can be ours through repentance and faith in Christ—all those things we have been talking about in this study—came alive to Wilberforce. He was born again. He changed from just another nameless wit haunting the environs of London, always on the lookout for what benefited himself, to Wilberforce the Great Liberator, a man who committed his life to ending slavery in Britain.

It took him decades of work, but Wilberforce eventually managed to push bills through Parliament abolishing first the slave trade and then slavery itself. His life had been transformed. Wilberforce became the champion of liberty only after God had freed his own soul with the message of the Bible—with the good news of Jesus Christ.

Will You Believe the Scriptures?

The Bible is God's revelation of himself to us. In the Old Testament and New, he reveals himself to us through the promises he makes and keeps. And then he calls us to respond to him in trust. In the 1813 Baptist Catechism, a variation of the Westminster Shorter Catechism, question 6 reads:

> Q. What things are chiefly contained in the holy scriptures?

> A. The holy scriptures chiefly contain what man ought to believe concerning God, and what duty God requireth of man (2 Tim. 1:13; 3:15–16).

Paul points to the same duty to believe when he writes, "I am not ashamed of the gospel, because it is the power of God for the salvation of everyone who believes: first for the Jew, then for the Gentile" (Rom. 1:16).

The question for you is, will you believe? Will you turn your life over to him? Will you trust him for what he says? We need that time-lapse camera sometimes to show us that God is faithful, because sometimes—if we are honest—it feels as if our prayers are not answered. So step back and look at what God does through the pages of Scripture. You will begin to see that he is faithful, just as he was to Abraham when he called him to an unfamiliar land. Abraham did not understand everything God was doing; yet he believed God and followed his instructions. And God blessed him. He gave Abraham the gift of faith so that Abraham could come to know him.

Trust His Promises

God gives us the promises in his Word as well, and we are called to respond to them in trust. Unlike Adam and Eve in the garden of Eden, and much like Jesus in the garden of Gethsemane, we must hear and believe God's Word. When we do, we will be restored to the relationship with God for which we were made.

This is the hope in which we can trust, because this is the hope that will not disappoint. And this is the chief concern of the whole Bible, Old Testament and New: God's restored relationship with his people for his own glory and his own pleasure.

QUESTIONS FOR REFLECTION ON THE WHOLE BIBLE

1. As we considered at the beginning, the Bible has been the subject of numerous and varying opinions. What are several of the most prominent opinions of the Bible that people have today?

2. If the Bible is comprised of sixty-six different books and has more than thirty different human authors, how could it possibly have one overarching storyline and one message?

3. What are some of the advantages of examining the whole Bible and its message in one fell swoop?

4. We have observed that the Bible is not only a book of wise religious counsel and theological propositions, though it has both. It is a story, a real story set in real history. Why do you think God might have revealed himself within a historical narrative? What advantages does that give us as readers?

5. What is atonement? How does the Old Testament link atonement and sacrifice? Were the sacrifices of the Old Testament effective in reconciling man to God?

6. What is the "riddle" of the Old Testament?

7. Suppose a Christian friend told you that he struggles with the God of the Old Testament because he

just seems so angry and wrathful. How would you respond?

8. How does Christ solve the riddle of the Old Testament? What do we mean when we refer to Christ as our "priest"?

9. What is the Christian gospel?

10. What do Christians have awaiting them at the consummation of all creation? What will Christians fully enjoy that was last enjoyed by Adam in the garden and partially by the high priest in the Most Holy Place? What do you think that will be like? Do you think you will grow tired of it? Can you imagine anything so beautiful and wonderful and marvelous that you would never grow tired of it?

11. If you were sitting in an undergraduate philosophy class—or wherever you happen to sit among non-Christians these days—and someone asked what the point of life is, what would you say? Could you defend your answer?

12. William Wilberforce seemed to take seriously Paul's own dilemma: "I desire to depart and be with Christ, which is better by far; but it is more necessary for you that I remain in the body" (Phil. 1:23–24). Wilberforce knew his prize awaited him in heaven, and so he was free to spend himself entirely on earth for God's work. Where is your ultimate prize? You prize something the most. You can figure out what it is by asking what you spend all your physical, financial, social, and mental resources trying to build, protect, or accomplish. What is it? Is your life increasingly lining up with the great promise of the Scriptures—or with something else?

THE MESSAGE OF THE OLD TESTAMENT: PROMISES MADE

CHAPTER EIGHT

IS THE OLD TESTAMENT REALLY WORTH READING?

I confess that I spend a good deal of time in bookstores. One of the trends I have noticed in secular bookstores over the last few years is to stock more and more religious books. Of course, the stores often classify them under "spirituality." Still, in this growing section you can browse through offerings on angels, warm thoughts, Ancient Eastern texts, the maxims of management gurus, and on and on in endless variety. Many of these books sell surprisingly well, too.

What do you think people are looking for in this blossoming spiritual book market? Guidance? Hope? Whatever the answer is, my guess is that comparatively few people would turn to the Old Testament.

You remember the Old Testament: "In the beginning" and all that! These words not only open the Bible, but they are probably the most famous words in the Old Testament, and perhaps one of the most well-known phrases in the English language.

Problems with the Old Testament

Yet it must be said that the majesty of this opening line has not endeared the Old Testament to many people. Many Christians and non-Christians alike consider the Old Testament too long and tedious, too obscure and cryptic. Besides, wasn't the Old Testament superseded by the New Testament? Studying the Old Testament compared to studying the New, some might think, would be like eating a fish with bones when you could have the boneless fillet, or like watching the big game from bad seats with a blocked view when you could be standing on the field.

Other people's problems with the Old Testament run a bit deeper. They will point to its frenzied prophets, its animal sacrifices, and its seemingly archaic laws and pejoratively label the whole thing as "primitive" or "crude." And, given that multiculturalism is the preeminent virtue of our own day, one could hardly find a book more out of step with the times than the Old Testament. One might say that it represents one of the worst displays of ethnocentrism in history.

Isn't this the book of the angry God who kills a man for trying to steady a decorated box, who sends bears to kill children for being disrespectful to their elders, who silences grumblers with deadly serpents simply for their grumbling?[1] Isn't this the book with divinely ordained threats and floods and hailstorms and fire and brimstone?

The wrath ascribed to God in this book does not make him seem grand or powerful to many people today. In fact, such wrath can tempt the most pious among us to regard him as

[1]Num. 21:4–9; 2 Sam. 6:6-9; 2 Kings 2:23–25.

arbitrary and cruel: a god who causes us not to worship, but to worry; an object not for admiration, but for abhorrence; the supreme embodiment not of beauty, but of ugliness. Well, now, we have gone and said it. And in a Christian book! I have heard people say such things in other places. So we might as well be honest in a Christian book that this is what many people think of the Old Testament.

Not New Problems

Such ideas are not new, of course. People have been embarrassed by the Old Testament throughout the history of the church. Toward the close of the second century, a man named Marcion and his followers broke off relations with other Christians. They rejected the entire Old Testament because its God seemed too cruel, wrathful, and inconsistent with the God revealed in Jesus of Nazareth. Of course, the Old Testament was the Bible of Jesus of Nazareth! (Marcion also accepted only the Gospel of Luke and ten of Paul's epistles from the New Testament.)

Though the church quickly and universally rejected Marcion's radical surgery of the Bible, the Old Testament has too often suffered a similar fate in our own circles of evangelical Christians. We don't make theological statements about it, but the effect is the same. Maybe we mine it for some good stories about Joseph, David, Moses, and Elijah. We may quote a couple of psalms, memorize several of the proverbs, and commend most of the Ten Commandments. But on the whole, we simply ignore it.

Our Plan for Understanding the Old Testament

Well, before we make the sweeping decision to omit such a large part of the Bible, I suggest that we should increase our understanding of what the Old Testament contains. And just as I did in our prior study over the whole Bible, I would like to summarize the Old Testament for you under three headings: first, a particular history; second, a passion for holiness; and third, a promise of hope.

I cannot deal with all the questions you might have about the Old Testament, but I can help with the framework, which we'll do over the next three chapters. Some people have summed up the message of the Old Testament as "God's people in God's place under God's rule." In a sense, that's similar to what I am suggesting. I would sum up the message of the Old Testament with the phrase "promises made." The promises God made in the Old Testament have been kept in the New, particularly in Jesus Christ.

As I said, the basic outline of the next three chapters will remain the same, and so some of the material you've already read will be repeated here. But most of it will be new since our goal is to drill deeper. What's our goal? I am convinced that if we can better understand the Old Testament, it will go a long way toward helping us understand the New Testament, which means we will better understand Christ, Christianity, God, and ourselves.

CHAPTER NINE

A PARTICULAR HISTORY

We will understand nothing about the Old Testament—or the God it reveals—if we do not understand that it is about a particular history. I know that I only have to say the word *history* and every other person will fall asleep. I know that history has a bad reputation as being quite boring. Perhaps in school you were taught to memorize long lists of dates and names. I am sorry about that. Not all of this chapter will be long lists of dates and names! Really, the story of the Old Testament is quite amazing.

The Storyline

Our text for this chapter begins, not surprisingly, on page 1 of your Bible: "In the beginning God created the heavens and the earth" (Gen. 1:1). Notice, this amazing story begins with nothing. And then the most extraordinary thing happens: from nothing we get something.

In that something, we see God's marvelous creative work. First, there is inanimate creation—water, earth, sun. Then God brings life—vegetation, fish, birds, animals. Perhaps you read in the newspapers about how excited scientists became when they thought they might have found water on the planet Mars, because where water exists, life exists. That might be exciting for secular people, but for Christians the most amazing thing is what God did next: he made people in his image, to reflect his character. All of this happens in the first two chapters of the Bible.

In the third chapter, God's first humans disobey him, and the whole cosmos falls into ruin as a consequence.

From chapters 4 to 6, we read a story of disintegration, beginning with the first son, Cain, who murders his brother, to the people of Noah's day, who are so bad that God decides to wipe out all the earth. You may think, "Maybe if we start over with just one righteous man and his family, human history will fare better." Of course, humanity did not fare better.

Beginning in chapter 10, the world is repopulated and then disintegrates again, epitomized by chapter 11's story of the Tower of Babel. At Babel, proud man tries to strike out independently from God, to which God responds with more judgment.

God then calls Abraham, in chapter 12, which marks yet another new beginning.

Before we get any further, we should note the vast scale of history contained in the Bible. I personally think that most of the history of the world may have happened before the days of Noah as recorded in Genesis 6. In the apostle Peter's second letter, he refers to the world before the flood as the "ancient world" or "the age that then was" (2 Pet. 2:5, author's translation). It's possible that whole empires that we have not even dreamed of rose and fell in the time before

Noah. Also, the time from Abraham to Jesus was as long as the time from Jesus to us today.

Anyway, God calls Abraham to be the first of God's new people. He gives Abraham descendants. Through Abraham's grandson, Jacob (also called Israel), God's people begin to experience prosperity. After a series of providential twists, these people end up as slaves in Egypt, yet they also quickly reproduce to become a vast nation.

Moses then brings the nation of Israel (named after Abraham's grandson) out of Egypt. God first gives Israel the law, which marks them off as his very special people. Second, he gives them the land he has promised, where this marked-off people are to live and display God's character to the nations. But instead of their displaying God's character, moral and political confusion follows during the rule of leaders called judges.

After some centuries, the people of Israel ask for and receive a king in the person of Saul, and then David follows Saul. David's reign best represents the archetype of a kingdom in which God's chosen man and God's Word rule over his people. The kingdom then arguably reaches its peak in the time of prosperity and the building of the temple by David's son Solomon. Yet Solomon becomes ungodly in many ways; and under Solomon's son Rehoboam, the kingdom divides in two. Both parts of the now-divided nation fall into idolatry, until God finally destroys the northern half through the Assyrian empire. A little over a century later, he exiles the southern half to Babylon. Several generations pass in exile, and then the people return and rebuild the temple and Jerusalem's wall. This is where Old Testament history ends, with the people reduced to a position of utter desperation and dependence on God.

This is the history recounted through the thirty-nine books of the Old Testament. The Old Testament is not just one book, you know, but thirty-nine smaller ones which, together, make up the whole.

The Thirty-nine Books

And these thirty-nine books are quite different. If you look at the table of contents in your Bible, you can distinguish the main categories. The first five books (Genesis to Deuteronomy) make up the Pentateuch, or the Law. The next twelve books (Joshua to Esther) are referred to as the Histories. Taken together, these first seventeen books form the narrative from creation to the return of the exiles from Babylon about four hundred years before Christ. The next five books (Job to Song of Solomon) are called the Writings. Then the last seventeen books are the Prophecies (Isaiah to Malachi). One way to divide the Christian canon of the Old Testament, then, would be to say there are seventeen books in the first group, five in the middle group, and seventeen in the last group. We will follow that division here.

HISTORICAL NARRATIVE

The first seventeen books of historical narrative (from Genesis to Esther) are fairly chronological. Yet the history of these books is not the dry history scholars write today that purports to be objective and balanced. No, it is confessional history. It is history written by people who know who God is and that they are his people.

- Genesis, as we have already said, describes how the world and the first humans were made. The garden of Eden presents the model of God and man living in perfect peace, which we will not see again until the final heavenly city in the New Testament book of Revelation. This peace is devastated by the fall, of course. God then initiates his plan of salvation through Abraham and his descendants. At the end of Genesis, God's people—the nation of Israel—are bound in slavery in Egypt.

- Exodus follows the history of God's people from the death of Joseph in Egypt through the exodus to the construction of the tabernacle in the wilderness, a building that symbolizes God's presence with his people. God uses Moses both to deliver the law and to deliver his people in the exodus.

- Leviticus presents a digest of God's laws given to his people in the wilderness. These laws highlight the problem of how sinful humans can approach a holy God. Holiness is the theme of the book of Leviticus.

- Numbers mostly tells the story of the people of Israel traveling to the Promised Land. It describes several dramatic instances of the people's unfaithfulness, together with God's persevering faithfulness.

- Deuteronomy is called Deuteronomy because it presents the second giving of the law (deutero = second; nomos = law). The people have reached the end of their forty-year wandering. The older generation has died off. So now God repeats the law for this new generation as they prepare to enter the Promised Land.

- Joshua describes the conquest of the Promised Land and its apportionment among the twelve tribes. The people were ruled by Moses' successor, Joshua.

- Judges comes next with the story of fourteen judges who ruled over Israel (or regions of Israel) after Joshua. The people continually reverted to lawlessness, and the times were well summed up by the phrase, "In those days Israel had no king; everyone did as he saw fit" (Judg. 21:25).

- Ruth is a little story set during the days of the judges. It functions as an Old Testament annunciation story, preparing the way for the birth of David.

- 1 and 2 Samuel are about the last judge, Samuel; a "false-start" king, Saul; and the first real king, David.

- 1 and 2 Kings turn the focus to the reign of David's son Solomon, followed by the fall of both Solomon and his line. The kingdom divides into two parts during the time of Solomon's son Rehoboam, and it's mostly downhill from there. Apart from several noteworthy revivals, both the northern and southern kingdoms gradually dissolve amid immorality and idolatry.

- 1 and 2 Chronicles present a kind of interesting summation of everything from Adam through the beginning of the exile. Their focus is on David, Solomon, the role of the temple, and then the kings of the southern kingdom leading up to the exile.

The last three books of history are about the exile and the return from exile:

- Ezra describes the return of the Jews from their captivity in Babylon and the rebuilding of the temple.
- Nehemiah continues the story by describing the rebuilding of Jerusalem's walls, a partial fulfillment of God's promises of restoration to his people.
- Esther is the last book of history. It is a story of God's providential deliverance of the Jewish community inside the Persian Empire late in the exile.

THE WRITINGS

The Old Testament's middle five books are known as the Writings, and they focus on some of the more personal experiences of the people of God. They are largely collections of wisdom literature, devotional poems, and ceremonial literature from the temple.

- Job is a story about a righteous man who is tried by God. We don't know when Job was written.
- The psalms are poetic prayers of praise, confession, and lament to God. Almost half of them appear to have been written by David. The collection was written over a wide span of time.
- Proverbs presents the wisdom of Solomon and others concerning the practical issues of life.
- Ecclesiastes, again probably by Solomon, recounts one man's search for the path to happiness and meaning in this world. It reads like the account of a man walking down the street at night, shining his flashlight down a

number of dead-end alleys and saying, "This is no good; this is no good; this is no good . . ."

- Song of Solomon is the collection of love songs between a bridegroom and his bride. It emphasizes the importance of loving relationships.

THE PROPHETS

The final collection of books in the Old Testament is the Prophets. If the first seventeen books present historical narrative, while the middle five books present the reflections of various individuals, this last group of seventeen presents God's commentary on Israel's history, particularly Israel's disobedience.

The first five books are called the Major Prophets because of their size; some of them are very long.

- Isaiah was a prophet in the southern kingdom, called Judah. The first thirty-nine chapters are composed of prophecies leading up to the captivity. Chapters 40 to 66 then point to a future restoration and redemption.
- Jeremiah uttered his prophecies in Jerusalem during the years the city was besieged, a siege that ended in the city's fall in 586 BC. He then continued to prophesy for seven years after the city's fall.
- Lamentations is the prophet Jeremiah's lament over Jerusalem's siege and destruction.
- Ezekiel prophesied in Babylon during this same time. He had actually been carried off from Jerusalem and taken to Babylon by Nebuchadnezzar in 597 BC. along

with a number of other Jews. Trained as a priest, Ezekiel prophesied against Judah up to the fall of Jerusalem, and then he turned to promising God's judgment on the nations and the restoration of God's people.

- Daniel, part prophecy and part history, chronicles the story of a Jewish captive in Babylon and how God used him in that place.

Following the five books of the Major Prophets are the twelve books of the Minor Prophets. They are called the Minor Prophets not because they lack importance but merely because they lack length.

- Hosea prophesied to the northern kingdom (generally called "Israel") at the same time that Isaiah prophesied to the southern kingdom. Hosea spoke of Israel's unfaithfulness, while God used Hosea's adulterous wife as a living example of how Israel had been unfaithful to God.
- Joel preached about the coming judgment of God on the southern kingdom. Then he promised that God's blessing would follow their repentance. (That's really the main theme for most of these prophets.)
- Amos predicted the judgment and restoration of Israel, the northern kingdom, while Isaiah was prophesying in the south.
- Obadiah uttered his very short prophecy of judgment against one of Judah's neighbors, Edom. He also promised restoration to the shattered Israelites.

- Jonah, when called to prophesy to the Assyrian city of Nineveh, fled and was swallowed by a great fish. In the belly of the fish, he prayed, repented, was delivered, and obeyed.

- Micah prophesied at the same time as Isaiah and Hosea. He spoke to both Israel and Judah concerning judgment and deliverance.

- Nahum, who lived about a century after Jonah, spoke out against Nineveh concerning the coming judgment of God. He also promised a future deliverance for Judah.

- Habakkuk reminded God's people living in a time of evil that God's judgment is certain, and that they can put their trust in his promise of restoration and ultimate protection.

- Zephaniah promised that judgment would come upon Judah. He also called them to repent, and he promised future blessing.

The last three prophets prophesied during the time of the rebuilding of Jerusalem under Ezra and Nehemiah.

- Haggai was a contemporary of Zechariah. He may have been born in captivity in Babylon, but he returned to Jerusalem and prodded the people to get on with rebuilding the temple.

- Zechariah, a contemporary of Haggai, prophesied two months after Haggai and presented a series of wild dreams that attacked the religious lethargy of the people and foresaw the messianic age.

- Malachi, perhaps a contemporary of Nehemiah in post-exilic Jerusalem, also attacked the religious apathy of the people and promised a coming Messiah. He was the last Old Testament prophet.

What History Teaches

All this history teaches that God picked a very specific people for himself. Some people feel that it is unfair for God to pick whom he wants. But let me remind you, God made the world. He can do as he pleases. He picked a people specifically to teach them who he is as God, what it means for him to be holy, and what it means for his people to be sinful and therefore dependent upon him and his mercy.

As we step back and look at the whole broad sweep, we find that we do not have some disembodied theology about the Lord; we have a very clear and specific earthy revelation of him. We observe God actually working with his people. We see what God is like, how people respond to him, and how he deals with them in turn. That brings us to the second thing to observe in the Old Testament, which we turn to next.

CHAPTER TEN

A PASSION FOR HOLINESS

We must understand not only the particular history of Israel, as we did in the last chapter, but we must also consider God's passion for holiness.

Like I said there, many people associate the Old Testament with an angry God, and they condemn him as unjust. It's true that God does become angry, but he becomes angry precisely because he is just! In short, I think that we will better understand God if we better understand his character.

Relationship through Covenants

When we Christians celebrate the Lord's Supper together, we often recite Jesus' words from the Gospels, "This cup is the new covenant in my blood." Jesus took this language of "covenant" straight out of the Old Testament, where the concept of a covenant is crucial. Now, maybe such covenant language sounds cold and legal to you, but in the Bible it isn't like that at all. It's the language of relationship! God's covenants were used to draw his people into a committed relationship with himself. And it is in the context of God's committed covenantal relationships that we find God's passion for holiness expressed.

In short, God was passionate for his covenanted people to be set apart unto him and to have characters and lives that were like his own. This is why sin is such a problem in the Bible, because sin is not like God. There is not the least trace of sin in God, and so it causes big problems for humans in relating to him. It separates God from us.

Anger at Sin

So does the Old Testament present a God who can be angry? Yes, but his expressions of anger are not whimsical tyranny. His anger expresses his commitment to his own holy character and his implacable opposition to human sin. Sin (the breaking of divine commandments) separates God's people from God and shows clearly their need to be reconciled to him.[1] God can be angry, in short, because he is not indifferent to sin and he is angry at the destruction of his creation.

The Old Testament explicitly teaches that all people are sinners,[2] and the storyline as a whole quickly leads to the conclusion that people are not able to deal with sin themselves (see Rom. 3:20; Gal. 2:16). Instead, the relationships that sin breaks require some sort of divinely initiated reparation. But how can this happen? Given God's holiness, how can peace with God be restored?

Atonement Leads to Reconciliation

This is where the biblical references to atonement become significant. The Anglo-Saxon word we use—*atonement*—means, quite literally, at-one-ment. Atonement must occur for two warring parties to be made at one.

---

[1]Prov. 15:29; Isa. 59:2; Hab. 1:13; Col. 1:21; Heb. 10:27.
[2]1 Kings 8:46; Ps. 14:3; Prov. 20:9; Eccles. 7:20; cf. Mark 10:18; Rom. 3:23.

The idea of offering an atoning act or ritual to placate an offended deity was not unique to ancient Israel; in fact, it was common among ancient religions. But the Old Testament authors uniquely placed the idea of atonement within the context of a relationship, and so they refer to the need for reconciliation in a way that was utterly unique in the ancient world.

Sacrifice Leads to Atonement

A number of images are used to describe atonement in the Old Testament. But the most prominent image God used to teach the people about atonement was sacrifice. Sinners could seek to restore their relationship with God through sacrifice.

Now, the picture of sacrifice given is not of a moody tribal deity who required the people to throw a young virgin into the volcano in order to be pacified. You will find this picture if you read about other ancient cultures—blind attempts to get some god to calm down by hurting yourself. But you won't find that idea in the Bible. In the Old Testament, God himself speaks and provides a way for propitiation—a way to turn his wrath aside and restore a rebellious people to himself.

In some ways, the idea of sacrifice almost seems innate. Shortly after Adam and Eve's eviction from the garden of Eden, their sons Cain and Abel offered sacrifices, even though God had not yet revealed the law. Abraham and his descendants offered sacrifices as well. Perhaps this innate compulsion to offer sacrifices, along with the ordinary habit of human mimicry, explains why sacrifices were so common among ancient religions.

Yet what's interesting about the Old Testament sacrifices, as we have already been suggesting, is how they differed from the sacrificial practices of the nations around them. Biblical sacrifices were not only for the grateful (to thank God for a wonderful harvest); and they certainly were not for the manipulative (to persuade God to send a good harvest). Instead, they were for the guilty—people who personally understood that they had violated God's commandments. Not only that, biblical sacrifices were not only for the ignorant person who thinks, "Maybe doing this will make things better." No, they were performed according to God's own instructions.

Specifically, God required the animals used as offerings to be without defect, to be costly, and to be voluntary by the person bringing the sacrifice.[3] The life of the unblemished animal victim, symbolized by its blood, would then be given in exchange for the life of the guilty human worshiper. In Exodus 12, for instance, the blood of the Passover lamb was given in exchange for a family's firstborn, who in turn represented the whole family. In Leviticus, God told the people, "The life of a creature is in the blood, and I have given it to you to make atonement for yourselves on the altar; it is the blood that makes atonement for one's life" (Lev. 17:11). Furthermore, the guilty human party in a Levitical sacrifice was required to place his or her hand on the head of the animal being sacrificed in order to indicate the transfer of guilt.

Sacrifices Teach

I know that the whole idea of such sacrifices is unpopular with many people—maybe they sound primitive and cruel. But can you see what God was teaching the people? First, he was teaching about his holiness and his passion for holiness.

[3]E.g., Gen. 9:5; Lev. 1:4; 4:4; 14:51; 16:21.

Second, he was teaching that sin is serious—deathly serious!—because it's such an aberration from his holiness.

And third, he was teaching that atonement could be accomplished when an innocent one dies in place of the guilty.

In and of themselves, Levitical sacrifices were never the point (as you can tell by Jeremiah's denunciations of what the people's sacrifices were leaving out; see Jer. 7:21ff.). Ironically, sacrifices were most appropriate when the person offering the sacrifice realized that the offering was not sufficient to atone for sins. So you have the psalmist saying, "Against thee, thee only, have I sinned" (Ps. 51:4 KJV). Sacrifices were not efficacious except by God's grace. They taught that sin defiles. They taught that sin physically hinders access to God. They taught that purification was needed. And they taught that sin is so serious that only death can make atonement.

Salvation and forgiveness would be costly.

The Day of Atonement

Both God's passion for holiness and the ultimately ineffective nature of sacrifices can be seen in the Old Testament through the Jewish Day of Atonement, a day on which a special sin offering was made for the whole nation. You can read about it in Leviticus 16.

Representing the people, the high priest entered the temple's Most Holy Place on one day of the year in order to offer a sacrifice in the very presence of God. First, he would make atonement for himself, since he too was a sinner. Then, he would make atonement for all the people. Who could see that blood offering that the high priest brought? No one but God! The high priest then confessed the sins of Israel over a second goat, which would be released outside the city in order to symbolize the total removal of sin by the penalty of being alienated, cast out, estranged from God's people.

It is particularly interesting that this ritual had to be repeated annually. Other nations would tend to offer sacrifices only when the nation was not prospering. But the Israelites were commanded to make sacrifice once a year regardless of the nation's situation. Why? God was teaching them that they were needy and separated from God, regardless of what had occurred in the nation's life. They regularly needed to make amends. They regularly needed to make atonement. They were in a state of sin, and no animal sacrifice could ultimately remove their guilt. There was no perfect sacrifice. If there had been, the people could have stopped offering them (Heb. 10:1–3). Instead, these imperfect sacrifices emphasized the fact that God is holy, that sin separates us from God, and that he provides a way for the forgiveness of sins and access to him.

A Riddle

This brings up the question that I have referred to as the "riddle" of the Old Testament. In Exodus 34, the Lord describes himself to Moses, saying "The LORD, the LORD, the compassionate and gracious God, slow to anger, abounding in love and faithfulness, maintaining love to thousands, and forgiving wickedness, rebellion and sin. Yet he does not leave the guilty unpunished" (Ex. 34:6–7a). Think about what God said: how can God both "forgive wickedness" and "not leave the guilty unpunished"?

There's one more thing we need to observe in our study of the Old Testament if we want to understand it and its God: the Old Testament's promise of hope. Thank goodness there's another chapter!

CHAPTER ELEVEN

A PROMISE OF HOPE

The Old Testament's picture of God is not one of grim condemnation. He is the same God we find in the New Testament. He is holy, just, and unwavering in his commitment to punish sin, but he is also a God of love, even toward his enemies.

God Commands Love

Does that surprise you? Many people are surprised when they hear that love is enjoined in the Old Testament. For instance:

- The great commandment given to Israel is, "Love the LORD your God with all your heart and with all your soul and with all your strength" (Deut. 6:5).
- The Lord commands the people to love their neighbors as themselves (Lev. 19:34). Jesus was quoting the Old Testament when he said this!
- God commands the Israelites to love foreigners because he does (Deut. 10:18–19).
- God even told the Israelites to return lost property to their enemies: "Do not gloat when your enemy falls;

when he stumbles, do not let your heart rejoice" (Prov. 24:17). And, "If your enemy is hungry, give him food to eat; if he is thirsty, give him water to drink" (Prov. 25:21).

All of this is from the Old Testament, and I could go on and on! I don't know which Old Testament you have been reading, but the real one is about love.

God Demonstrates Love

Now, this is one way we could try to demonstrate that the God of the Old Testament is the same God as the God of the New Testament—going through the text piece by piece and pointing to all the individual injunctions and examples of love. But even more convincing, I believe, is considering the whole sweep of history presented in the Old Testament, where we witness God's patience and loving forbearance toward creatures made in his image who nevertheless reject him. Why is Old Testament history so long? "He is patient with you, not wanting anyone to perish, but everyone to come to repentance," said the apostle Peter (2 Pet. 3:9).

God's forbearing love can be seen in the fact that he did not end human history right at the fall, when he would have been just to do so. Then throughout centuries and centuries of Israel's history, God patiently forbore with the wayward nation. Ultimately, the Old Testament presents God's grace, love, mercy, and patience on an epic scale.

God has always planned and promised to reveal his glory to his people. And so he did, throughout the Old Testament.

What Is the Promise of Hope?

What then is the promise of hope God's people can look to in the Old Testament? Clearly, their hope could not be in their own history. It was a history of repeated failure!

Nor, finally, could their hope be in the sacrificial system. As the psalmist said, "Sacrifice and offering you did not desire, but my ears you have pierced" (Ps. 40:6), meaning God made the psalmist his own. The authors of the Old Testament even seemed to understand what the author of Hebrews meant when he wrote:

> The law is only a shadow of the good things that are coming— not the realities themselves. For this reason it can never, by the same sacrifices repeated endlessly year after year, make perfect those who draw near to worship. If it could, would they not have stopped being offered? For the worshipers would have been cleansed once for all, and would no longer have felt guilty for their sins. But those sacrifices are an annual reminder of sins, because it is impossible for the blood of bulls and goats to take away sins. (Heb. 10:1–4)

An endlessly repeated sacrifice can't make people perfect. The blood of bulls and goats cannot take away sin. So where is there hope in all this?

Riddle Solved . . .

To find the answer, we have to return to Exodus 34 where we saw the riddle of the Old Testament. Remember, we asked, how can God both "forgive wickedness" and still "not leave the guilty unpunished"? After all, you and I both deserve

God's punishment, no matter how virtuous you might think you are for persevering through a chapter on the entire Old Testament! We all stand guilty before God. And Exodus 34 promises that God will not leave our sin unpunished. So what hope is there?

Atonement requires, we said, a substitution of suffering and death by an innocent party on behalf of the guilty party. But, we have also suggested, it takes more than the death of an animal to accomplish this. Some relationship between the victim and the guilty is required, a relationship far closer than what's possible between us and an animal who is not made in God's image.

The answer to the Old Testament riddle for the Israelites and for us could never be in ourselves or in a lamb. Their hope and ours has to be in the Old Testament's promised person.

. . . In the Anointed One—the Messiah

People in Jesus' day did not wonder whether a Messiah would come. They took it for granted that their only hope was in the specially "anointed one" of God. But when this anointed one came, his manner of coming took everyone by surprise. He—Jesus—presented himself as fulfilling not just the Old Testament promises of a kingly Messiah but also another set of promises—the promise of the Lord's servant who would come to suffer for his people in their stead.

Jesus brought together the Old Testament prophecies of the Messiah-King and the prophecies of the Lord's servant who would suffer for his people. Obviously, Jesus had meditated on the Old Testament deeply and knew these words from Isaiah:

> Surely he took up our infirmities
>   and carried our sorrows,
> yet we considered him stricken by God,
>   smitten by him, and afflicted.
> But he was pierced for our transgressions,
>   he was crushed for our iniquities;
> the punishment that brought us peace was upon him,
>   and by his wounds we are healed.
> We all, like sheep, have gone astray,
>   each of us has turned to his own way;
> and the LORD has laid on him
>   the iniquity of us all. (Isa. 53:4–6)

This promise points to the answer to the riddle of the Old Testament. This promise is the hope of the Old Testament. In fact, what the Old Testament teaches us more than anything is that this promise is our only hope at all!

QUESTIONS FOR REFLECTION ON THE OLD TESTAMENT

1. How would you describe the Old Testament compared to the New? How much time have you spent studying the Old Testament? What essential lessons about the Christian life have you learned from it?

2. Why is reading, studying, and understanding the history of God's work with his people in the Old Testament helpful, even essential, for understanding who God is? What dangers do we risk by failing to understand how God has worked in history?

3. Is the God of the Old Testament an angry God? More angry than the God of the New Testament?

4. Is there any sense in which a Christian should be grateful for and find comfort in the fact that God becomes angry over sin? Why?

5. Did the Old Testament sacrifices remove the guilt of the person bringing the sacrifice? What purpose did the Passover sacrifice and the Levitical sacrifices serve?

6. Why would it benefit a Christian to spend time studying and meditating upon Old Testament sacrifices such as the Passover, or even the entire book of Leviticus?

7. What's the riddle of the Old Testament? What's the answer to the riddle?

8. Why was the manner in which Jesus came and presented himself as the Messiah surprising? Why is it hope-giving?

9. Why should the average Christian spend more time reading, studying, and meditating on the Old Testament?

THE MESSAGE OF THE NEW TESTAMENT: PROMISES KEPT

CHAPTER TWELVE

WHERE DO YOU SET YOUR HOPES?

In 1858, the Illinois legislature elected Stephen A. Douglas to the office of U.S. senator instead of Abraham Lincoln. Afterward, a sympathetic friend asked Lincoln how he felt, to which he responded, "Well, a little bit like the boy who stubbed his toe; I am too big to cry and too badly hurt to laugh."

As a pastor on Capitol Hill, I am struck every election season by how one person's political victory is someone else's political loss. No matter who wins an election, a vast number of people—up to half—are disappointed. People become so involved in partisan politics that election seasons can be a time of great hope for some and, just as surely, great disappointment for others.

Sometimes we can bear disappointment well. Some people are so given over to disappointment they actually seem to thrive on it. Like the character Eeyore in the Winnie-the-Pooh tales, they take comfort in looking for the dark cloud around every silver lining. For most of us, however, disappointment can feel like a sharp thrust to the heart. We do what we can just to get by.

The Difficulty of Hope

Did you ever see the movie *Shadowlands*—the story about
C. S. Lewis's late-in-life marriage to Joy Davidman? In an
opening scene of the movie, Lewis is sitting amid several of
his students at Oxford and he refers to a piece of poetry that
mentions the image of a perfect rosebud. Lewis asks what the
image of the bud represents. One of the students responds,
"Love?"

"What kind of love?" asks Lewis impatiently.

"Untouched," says a student.

"Unopened, like a bud?" asks another student.

"Yes, more?"

Another student says anxiously, "Perfect love."

"What makes it perfect?" asks Lewis, "Come on, wake
up."

"Is it the courtly ideal of love?"

Now, that is a little inside Lewis joke, because Lewis had
written a thesis on the courtly ideal of love. Still, Lewis replies,
"Okay, what is that, though? What is the courtly ideal's one
essential quality?"

The students are quiet. They don't know the answer. So
Lewis himself answers: "Unattainability. The most intense
joy lies not in the having, but in the desiring. The delight that
never fades. Bliss that is eternal is only yours when what you
most desire is just out of reach."

Well, is that true? It sounds fine as an artistic and romantic
ideal, but is life like that? Is the only lasting bliss the bliss of
desire rather than fulfillment? If so, how can we have hope
without the possibility of actually attaining that for which we
hope? After all, the pain of disappointment is acute because the

object of our desires comes close and then we miss it. Whether it is a lost election, a collapsed business scheme, a disproved theory, a canceled vacation, a piece of defeated legislation, a failed job prospect, or a departed loved one, we understand what the writer of the proverb means when he says, "Hope deferred makes the heart sick" (Prov. 13:12). In other words, we cannot overlook what our hearts are set upon.

What do you set your hopes upon? If you cannot answer that question, you may not be able to benefit from the rest of this study. It is crucial for you and me both to answer that question: What are our hopes set upon? Many of our problems come from attaching our hopes to things that were not made to bear them. Some things hold out great promise but they prove to be passing fancies as life goes on. Other things are actually dangerous and destructive. In this old world, it is not only in politics that promises made are not necessarily promises kept.

Of course, this is where God comes in. As the one who made us, he knows how we work best. He knows what we should hope for, and he has set those very things in the Bible so that we can fix our hopes upon them.

Our Plan for Understanding the New Testament

In the last section of this book, "The Message of the Old Testament: Promises Made," we looked at the "big picture" of the Old Testament. Now we will do a similar overview of the New Testament. As I mentioned at the beginning of our study of the Old Testament, you will find that the outline here repeats the outline of our overview of the whole Bible, so some of the material will be repeated. Still, our goal is to drill deeper, that we might better understand the hope to which we've been called.

In the Old Testament, we saw that God created the earth and then patiently bore with a people who rebelled against him. Beginning with Abraham, he chose a special people of his own. Those people, the nation of Israel, waxed and waned for almost two millennia until their once high hopes almost vanished when their nation was crushed a final time by an alien invader—the mighty Roman Empire. When this final defeat occurred, they felt disappointed to the point of heartsickness and despair. Would their deliverer never come? Would they never be restored to the fellowship with God for which they longed? Would the world never be put right?

The New Testament tells the story of how all the promises made in the Old Testament were actually kept. And as we understand what God is doing in the grand scheme of history, our own disappointments and hopes will begin to fall into perspective.

In order to view the whole New Testament, we will look first at Christ, then at God's covenant people, and finally at the renewal of all of creation. Think of three concentric circles. First, we focus on Christ; then we expand outward to the new-covenant people; and, finally, we take in all creation.

CHAPTER THIRTEEN

CHRIST

The first question that must be addressed concerning the New Testament is, did the deliverer whom God promised in the Old Testament actually come?

The New Testament answers that Old Testament question with a resounding yes! And he is not just an ordinary human deliverer; he is God come in the flesh. The one and only Son, Jesus, perfectly displayed the Father, so that God's people might know him and be delivered from their sins. The New Testament squarely focuses on Christ. He is the heart of it all. He is the center of its message.

God has always had a plan for creation. Before history even began, the New Testament teaches, God planned to send his Son as a human to die for the sins of his people. After God created the universe and humankind, Adam and Eve rebelled against God's rightful rule. God then called a special people to himself in Abraham. Through Abraham's descendent Jacob, or Israel, the family grew to be a great nation. The majority of this nation was then destroyed by invading armies because of its sin, while the survivors were taken captive, exiled, dispersed, and only partly regathered from exile. Yet God's plan remained firmly in place through all of this. In this tattered remnant would be found the coming deliverer, the anointed one—in Hebrew, the "Messiah"; in Greek, the "Christ."

The Four Gospels and Acts

The collection of twenty-seven books that comprise the New Testament begins with four accounts of the life of this Messiah—Jesus of Nazareth. Look at the contents page in your Bible. Under the New Testament heading you will see four books at the top of the list—Matthew, Mark, Luke, and John. Following these four is a fifth—Acts. All five of these books argue that Jesus of Nazareth is the Messiah.

These books are documentaries, as it were, of Jesus' life, and they make the case for his messiahship. They presented to their readers the tremendous news that the promised deliverer had actually come! The one for whom God's people were waiting had come! Where Adam and Israel had failed and been unfaithful, Jesus proved faithful. He survived the temptations. He lived a life without sin. Furthermore, Jesus fulfilled God's promise to Moses of a coming prophet (Deut. 18:15, 18–19). Jesus fulfilled God's promise to David of a coming king (2 Sam. 7:12–13). Jesus fulfilled the prophecy of the divine son of man witnessed by Daniel (Dan. 7:13–14). All of these promises and more were fulfilled, say these four Gospels, in Jesus of Nazareth. In fact, according to John chapter 1, Jesus was the Word of God made flesh—God himself living in human form.

Turning to these Gospels individually, we note that Matthew was probably written for a Jewish community. He stresses Jesus' fulfillment of Old Testament prophecies, such as the many prophecies about his birth. Matthew includes five major teaching sections, each of which shows Jesus to be the great prophet promised by Moses.

Mark chronicles, perhaps, the apostle Peter's recollections. The book does not say that, but various things in the book make us think Mark compiled Peter's recollections about Jesus for the Roman Christians, maybe around the time Peter was killed for being a Christian. Seeing the first apostles killed, the church may have wanted to commit these things to writing. Mark's account is the shortest of all the Gospels, and it may be the oldest.

Luke, the third Gospel, is sometimes called the Gospel to the Gentiles. Luke stresses that the Messiah has come not just for the Jewish people but for all the nations of the world, and he puts to good use the Old Testament prophecies that make this promise. Luke also wrote a second volume, the book of Acts. Acts is "part two" of Luke's work. It shows how Jesus actively expanded his church through his Spirit. So even after Jesus' crucifixion, resurrection, and ascension, his work continued as the church grew and as God established this new society. Luke concluded his narrative with Paul imprisoned—but still ministering—in Rome.

The fourth book is the Gospel of John, which may be the most beloved of the Gospels. It is different from the other three Gospels in some ways. It does not teach a different theology but it has an especially clear emphasis on both Jesus' identity as the Messiah and the fact that the Messiah is God himself. John explicitly states this purpose for his Gospel in chapter 20: "These are written that you may believe that Jesus is the Christ [that is, the Messiah], the Son of God, and that by believing you may have life in his name" (20:31).

Jesus Is the Promised Messiah

These are the four Gospels and the book of Acts. They begin the New Testament by showing us that the promises made about the Messiah—the Christ—in the Old Testament have been fulfilled in Jesus.[1] They proclaim the good news that God has kept his promises to deliver not just his Old Testament people but you and me as well, if we repent of our sins and follow his Son.

If the collection of the Gospels and Acts strikes you as just a few more musty old history books, you have not read them very well. Read them again. I think you will find there is more than you suspect, even as I did when I began reading them carefully as an agnostic. The Gospels show that Jesus the Messiah is not just the Lord of people who lived two thousand years ago but is the Lord that you need in your life.

[1]Among many other designations, Jesus is also described as the New Adam (2 Cor. 15:45–47); the Righteous One (Acts 3:14; 1 John 2:1); greater than Moses (John 1:17; 5:45–46; Heb. 3:1–6); and greater than David (Matt. 22:41–45; Acts 2:29–36). Abraham also rejoiced to see his day (John 8:56–58).

CHAPTER FOURTEEN

A NEW-COVENANT PEOPLE

Christ is at the heart of the New Testament's message, as we just considered, and then we move outward to his special covenant people. This is the second concentric circle in understanding the message of the New Testament.

Glimpses of Christ's work among his people can be seen in the Gospels, especially among the disciples. Yet it really picks up momentum in the book of Acts and then in the New Testament Epistles. God himself took on human form in order to display his image in Jesus Christ, as we see in the Gospels. Yet the Old Testament teaches that God made human beings—all of us—in his image to display his image to creation. So as we read along in the New Testament, the transforming, image-clarifying work of Christ among his special covenant people emerges as a second dominant theme.

A New Covenant

Now, I know the word *covenant* is not used very often these days. If anything, it sounds like a legal term. In our study of the Old Testament, we thought about the "covenant" language used in ancient Israel and we found that it is not cold, legal language; it is the language of relationship. Then in the Gospels Jesus used the language of covenant when he shared the Last Supper with his disciples: "This cup is the new covenant in my blood, which is poured out for you" (Luke 22:20). Covenants are used to form new relationships, which is why Jesus came: to make a new relationship for his people with God, because that relationship had been destroyed by sin.

Jesus said very strangely, toward the beginning of John, "Destroy this temple, and I will raise it again in three days" (John 2:19). At the time, he was standing in the temple in Jerusalem; but then he told his disciples he was talking about his body (2:21–22). He himself was the temple that would be destroyed and rebuilt. He would be the new meeting place for God and his people, just as the temple in Jerusalem had been in former days. He would be the mediator between God and man. As we have already considered, Jesus Christ fulfilled the Old Testament promise that the Messiah would come as a prophet and a king. But in order to deliver his people from their sin and establish his new covenant, Jesus also fulfilled the promise that the Messiah would come as a priest. Like the Levitical priests of the Old Testament, he would intercede between God and man with a blood sacrifice. The rescue needed by God's people, ultimately, was a rescue from their sins.

A Substitute for Sin

The Old Testament temple, priests, and sacrifices could not effectually accomplish (and were never intended to accomplish) that work of intercession and reconciliation, which brings us once again to the riddle of the Old Testament. In Exodus 34 God revealed himself as the Lord who "forgives wickedness" (see 34:7). Then in the same sentence, he said he "will not leave the guilty unpunished." The riddle, we have said, is this: how can God "forgive wickedness" and yet "not leave the guilty unpunished"? The Levitical priests could not solve the riddle by sacrificing bulls and goats (Heb. 10:4). The answer to the riddle is found, of course, in Jesus. Jesus came as priest, sacrifice, temple, and substitute, in order to intercede between God and man by taking upon his body God's punishment for sin. God could then forgive the wickedness of his people and yet ensure that their wickedness is punished. The New Testament provides the answer to the riddle posed in the Old. Jesus' death on the cross allowed God to both forgive and punish. Christ forms the new covenant—he reestablishes a relationship between God and his people—with his blood.

Not that the Old Testament did not foresee this. Through the prophet Isaiah, the Lord promised:

> Surely he took up our infirmities
>   and carried our sorrows,
> yet we considered him stricken by God,
>   smitten by him, and afflicted.
> But he was pierced for our transgressions,
>   he was crushed for our iniquities;
> the punishment that brought us peace was upon him,
>   and by his wounds we are healed.
> We all, like sheep, have gone astray,
>   each of us has turned to his own way;
> and the LORD has laid on him
>   the iniquity of us all. (Isa. 53:4–6)

Isaiah said these things centuries before the birth of Christ. Yet that is exactly what God did for us in Christ!

It is clear from the Gospels that Jesus had meditated on the Isaiah passage and knew he would fulfill those very prophecies. So he taught his disciples, "The Son of Man did not come to be served, but to serve, and to give his life as a ransom for many" (Mark 10:45). After his resurrection, "beginning with Moses and all the Prophets, he explained to them what was said in all the Scriptures concerning himself." He also told them, "This is what is written: The Christ will suffer and rise from the dead on the third day, and repentance and forgiveness of sins will be preached in his name to all nations, beginning at Jerusalem" (Luke 24:27, 46–47).

A Righteous People

Notice, the good news is not simply that Christ came; it's that Christ came to save a guilty people and make them clean.

The very thing the letter of Hebrews says never happened in the Old Testament has now come to pass in the New. In the Old Testament, God's people were only ceremonially clean. The covenant in the Old Testament was real, but partial. The prophets knew this and promised that a new covenant would come. Speaking through the prophet Jeremiah, God said:

> "The time is coming," declares the LORD,
>   "when I will make a new covenant
> with the house of Israel
>   and with the house of Judah.
> It will not be like the covenant
>   I made with their forefathers
> when I took them by the hand
>   to lead them out of Egypt,
> because they broke my covenant,
>   though I was a husband to them," declares the LORD.

> "This is the covenant I will make with the house of Israel
>   after that time," declares the LORD.
> "I will put my law in their minds
>   and write it on their hearts.
> I will be their God,
>   and they will be my people. . . .
> For I will forgive their wickedness
>   and will remember their sins no more." (Jer. 31:31–33,
>   34b)

Now, in the New Testament, God finally has a people who are not just ceremonially clean; the guilt of their sins has actually been removed because of Christ's death on the cross.

As Christians, we are counted as completely righteous in Christ, and we are being made holy in our lives today, as attested to by our manner of living and interactions with one another. We are not perfect by any means. If you have any doubt about that, get a mirror. Nevertheless, we are growing and improving with the help of God, dealing with life in a way that brings him glory and honor, not pretending we have no disappointments, but knowing where to turn in those disappointments and where to set our hopes. God is making us his own, and we wait for the completion of his work. For on that day, we will be fully, finally, and personally holy in the way that we are now holy in Christ.

In all this, a Christian's salvation is past, present, and future. So Paul can tell the Ephesian Christians they have been saved (Eph. 2:8–9), the Corinthian Christians they are being saved (1 Cor. 1:18), and the Roman Christians they shall be saved (Rom. 5:9). This accomplished, ongoing, and promised salvation distinguishes the covenanted people of God from the rest of humanity.

THE PAULINE AND GENERAL EPISTLES

What all this means occupies almost the rest of the New Testament. If you look back at the table of contents for the New Testament, you will see the first four Gospels. Following these is the book of Acts, which is really the transition from these Gospels to the books about living as God's people. In Acts, the gospel expands outward from Jerusalem, to Judea, to Samaria, and, with Paul's three missionary journeys, to the ends of the world. After Acts, the rest of the New Testament books are letters written to early Christians about what it means to live as the special covenant people of God, who are distinct from the rest of the world.

PAUL'S EPISTLES

The first thirteen letters were written by the apostle Paul, a former rabbi and Pharisee who was remarkably converted by God while traveling to persecute some Christians "to their death," as he puts it (Acts 22:4). His letters are ordered in the New Testament from longest to shortest—first, letters to churches, and then, letters to individuals. In his first letter, Romans, Paul explains that God has been faithful to his covenant through Christ. Through Christ, God has provided a righteousness for his people, which is accounted to us by faith, as was the case with Abraham.

Then 1 and 2 Corinthians were written to a church with a lot of troubles. The church lived within a very secular society, so Paul tried to help them sort out how to live holy, special, distinct lives in an unholy culture. You will find a lot of very interesting parts in these two letters, such as a famous chapter on love (1 Corinthians 13). In the second letter to the Corinthians, Paul passionately defends his own ministry.

If you want just the sharp edge of Paul's teaching, Galatians is a good summary. He is clear about what he is saying, and he is clear about what he is not saying.

Then in Ephesians Paul writes about the church God is creating. God had always planned to create the church, and it is a new society calling together both Jews and Gentiles in Christ.

Philippians—often called the happiest book in the New Testament because Paul does not seem to have a cross word to say—encourages its readers to rejoice in the Lord. It includes that beautiful hymn in chapter 2 describing how Christ, though being equal with God, made himself nothing and gave himself to die on the cross (Phil. 2:6–11).

Colossians is about Christ's supremacy over all and some implications this has for our lives.

First and Second Thessalonians are two of Paul's earliest letters. Apparently, a number of people in Thessalonica had heard about Christ's second coming and, misunderstanding it, had quit their jobs. They were just hanging around like fanatics, waiting for God to do something. So Paul writes and tells them to get a job.

Next are Paul's personal letters, written to his individual friends. Paul wrote 1 and 2 Timothy to Timothy, a young minister he discipled and trained. The letters were intended to encourage this young associate in his work as an elder. Second Timothy is probably the last letter Paul ever wrote.

The letter to Titus was written to a ministerial friend Paul had left on the island of Crete to establish elders in the new churches and to complete other unfinished business.

Finally, Paul wrote a very short letter to Philemon, which you could easily read in the next five minutes. Philemon was the owner of an escaped slave who had found Paul and become a believer. It is interesting to see how Paul deals with a slave owner.

THE GENERAL EPISTLES

The rest of the New Testament is comprised of a second set of letters, none of which were written by Paul. There are nine of them, and again they are basically in order of length.

The author of the first letter in this second set, Hebrews, is unknown. Hebrews helps us understand the relationship between the Old and New Testaments as well as what it means for us to be the new-covenant people of God. Evidently some Christians were considering going back to some version of the older covenant God had made with Moses. After all, these plain Christian assemblies meeting in people's homes, devoid of any great ceremony, felt unimpressive. Back in the temple in Jerusalem, there was incense, sacrifices, fancy garments, great horns, and so forth. All that felt special, maybe even religiously satisfying. So people were beginning to turn back. The author of Hebrews responded by saying, in essence, "Look very carefully. Under the old covenant, you have priests who died because of their own sin. And their endless sacrifices of bulls and goats made people only ceremonially clean. But look at what you have in Christ! The eternal, sinless Son of God gave himself once forever to make his people truly clean and holy. The blood of the former sacrifices merely points to him."

James is a very practical letter. He describes how to live the Christian life with a practical concern for others.

First and Second Peter are relevant for the church today because they were written to Christians who were beginning to undergo difficulties for being Christians. This confused them. I think they were assuming, "If I am living rightly, won't life go well?" Peter responded, "Actually, if you look at the life of Jesus, you will see this is not a good assumption. In fact, living rightly can mean life does not go well, at least not in this world." Both of these letters encourage Christians to persevere in the faith, with Christ as their example. The second letter also warns about the danger of false teachers.

First, Second, and Third John are three brief letters written to encourage Christians in their lives of love and faithful obedience to the Lord.

Jude is a brief letter, similar to 2 Peter, warning against false and immoral teachers.

These are the New Testament's instructions for us about what it means to be the covenant people of God. In the New Testament, the promises made to the holy people in the Old Testament are kept in God's new-covenant people. If we are Christians, they are kept in us today.

The Good News

What's the good news of the New Testament? Christ did not come for himself; he came for his people. As you read through the whole New Testament, you will not only find that Jesus is the Messiah, but you will find what this means for you. As Paul wrote, "God sent his Son, born of a woman, born under law, to redeem those under law, that we might receive the full rights of sons" (Gal. 4:4–5). Christ came to make a people for himself.

One of the New Testament's most amazing passages is Revelation 5. The apostle John is given a vision of the great throne room of God in heaven. As John looks, God's decrees for the rest of history are brought into the room on a scroll. John desperately wants to know what history contains. What has God decreed? But the scroll is sealed, so he begins to weep.

An elder approaches John and says, "Do not weep! See, the Lion of the tribe of Judah, the Root of David, has triumphed. He is able to open the scroll and its seven seals" (Rev. 5:5). John looks up to see this Lion of the tribe of Judah, this mighty king of the beasts, but what does he see? "Then I saw a Lamb, looking as if it had been slain, standing in the center of the throne" (5:6). The ferocious lion that God sends to devour his enemies is a Lamb that he sends to be slain.

This is not the way you or I would have rescued a people. If we had been made director and producer of the messianic coming, we would have sent somebody who would clean up in the polls, who would win all his battles, and who would bring everything our flesh desired. But that is not the way God did it. The enemy to be devoured is sin. So he sent a sacrifice to die on our behalf. The Lion of the tribe of Judah is the Lamb that was slain.

God would be completely justified to leave us all eternally separated from him in hell under the penalty of our sin, yet in his great love, God has not done that. He sent his Son, who came and lived a perfect life and who therefore deserved no wrath or punishment for sin. Christ died on the cross specifically to take the place of everyone who turns and trusts in him. In exchange for our sinfulness, we are given his holiness. In Christ, then, we are declared holy before God and are brought into a reconciled, everlasting relationship with him. That is good news!

CHAPTER FIFTEEN

A NEW CREATION

In many church services you will hear the prayer, "Thy kingdom come. Thy will be done on earth as it is in heaven." Have you ever wondered what that means? It falls off our tongues so easily. Many of us have said it since childhood: "Thy kingdom come. Thy will be done on earth as it is in heaven."

Stop Limiting Your Hopes

Consider for a moment the kind of people who carefully tend their hearts because they want to avoid hurt or disappointment. The only hopes they allow themselves are the hopes they are able to make happen. The only promises they hear or make to themselves are the promises they have the power to keep.

Yet limiting your hopes in this fashion is the complete opposite of Christianity. If you tend your heart in this way, I encourage you to look at the gospel. As Christians, Peter says, "we are looking forward to a new heaven and a new earth, the home of righteousness" (2 Pet. 3:13), and this is entirely beyond our power to effect. No elected party, no economic scheme, no job promotion, and no successful relationship can bring about the great thing we as Christians wait for. We wait for the fulfillment of our first and final hope: the whole world being put right, as God's plan in the New Testament extends from Christ to his covenant people to the outermost circle—his whole creation.

In other words, we wait for his kingdom to come and his will to be done, on earth as it is in heaven.

The Book of Revelation

This is what we find at the end of the New Testament in the book of Revelation. It is a letter too, but it is an unusual letter in which the apostle John describes a number of visions God gave him. In certain respects, John's apocalyptic letter picks up on the Old Testament prophetic tradition by focusing on great events that lie in store for the earth's inhabitants. More specifically, Revelation describes the consummation of God's people, in God's place, in right relationship to him. The church militant becomes the church triumphant—the victorious church in heaven. And the whole heavens and earth are re-created forever (see Rev. 21:1–4; 21:22–22:5).

The Bible does not present Christians as Platonists or gnostics—people who think this world and material things do not matter, that only the spiritual afterlife matters. Throughout the book of Revelation and the whole New Testament, the biblical authors stress the bodily nature of the resurrection. Jesus was bodily resurrected, and his resurrection is called "the firstfruits." It begins what we will experience in the final resurrection from the dead. We will be taken up to be with God forever, but that is no world-denying proposition. God's plan for the world does not exist on some ethereal plain, far away from concrete reality. There is an interesting verse in Revelation that reads: "The nations will walk by [Christ's] light, and the kings of the earth will bring their splendor into" the city of heaven (Rev. 21:24). In the final consummation of creation, the kings of the earth will present their splendors and all the cultural grandeur of the world before the gathered heavenly assembly; and all these things will display God's glory as we discover what he meant for creation. Not only what Mark the preacher or Mary the Sunday school teacher brings will be counted worthwhile. Rather, the things you and I do in our daily lives in business, education, government, health care, or our families—if we have done them unto the Lord—will be presented and appear on the last day as adding to the luster of God's glory. These things are part of God's plan for the world.

And here at the end, the holiness of God's people will finally be complete, as they are at home with him. John wrote in his first letter, "Dear friends, now we are children of God, and what we will be has not yet been made known. But we know that when he appears, we shall be like him, for we shall see him as he is" (1 John 3:2). The end will be like the beginning, only better. The garden of Eden, in some sense, will be restored. God will dwell with his people. The whole heavenly city is presented in Revelation as a perfect cube, which recalls the Most Holy Place in the Old Testament temple. The Most Holy Place, which represented the presence of God on earth, was also in the shape of a cube. Only now, this heavenly cube is not restricted to the high priests once a year, as in ancient Israel; all the children of God will enter his presence, and we will live there with him forever! That is how the book called the New Testament ends.

The Curtain Drops

It is a good way for the New Testament to end, I think. It gives us as Christians great news to offer the world. We presently live in a time of waiting, but we wait with God and we wait for God. After all, Revelation was written by a man in his nineties who had been exiled on an island by the mightiest power on earth, the Roman Empire. At the time, Christians were being killed for their faith. He was utterly desperate and dependent upon God. Yet he was full of hope because his hope did not rest on external circumstances. It rested on the sovereign God who ruled above the Roman emperors. That's when the curtain of the New Testament drops.

God promises in Scripture that the earth will be filled with the knowledge of his glory, and the promise is certain to be kept in his new creation.

Promises made, promises kept.

THE MAKER AND KEEPER OF PROMISES

Of course, some disappointments have their uses. The ruins of our own cherished plans often become the steps we take toward the true good that God has waiting for us. Some of the very things you hope for right now are what God in his great love wants to pry from your fingers so that you can receive what is better from him.

Paul learned that when he prayed three times for God to remove the thorn from his flesh. God told Paul that his strength would be made perfect in Paul's weakness. So Paul rejoiced to become weak for the glory of God.

And this is what we find in our own lives. When we cling to the world with all our might, we soon realize we cannot hold on. As Jesus said, "What good is it for a man to gain the whole world, yet forfeit his soul?" (Mark 8:36). God has something even better than the whole world for his children.

When Every Chapter Is Better Than the Last

In the last paragraph of the last book of C. S. Lewis's series *The Chronicles of Narnia*, Lewis captures something of the nature of Christian hope. He writes:

> And as Aslan spoke, he no longer looked to them like a lion; but
> the things that began to happen after that were so great and
> beautiful that I cannot write them. And for us this is the end of
> all the stories, and we can most truly say that they all lived hap-
> pily ever after. But for them it was only the beginning of the real
> story. All their life in this world and all their adventures in Narnia
> had only been the cover and the title page: now at last they were
> beginning Chapter One of the Great Story which no one on earth
> has read: which goes on forever: in which every chapter is better
> than the one before.[1]

After considering the mysteries of God, his mercies to us
in Christ, and the hope we have as his covenant children,
Paul dissolves into doxology and says, "Oh, the depth of
the riches of the wisdom and knowledge of God! How unsearchable his judgments, and his paths beyond tracing out!"
(Rom. 11:33).

Who Will Trust? Who Will Believe?

So I hope I have been clear: the point of the New Testament,
indeed, the point of the whole Bible, is that God has made
promises to us, he has kept those promises to us, and we are
called to trust him because he is the keeper of promises! God
has revealed himself to humanity through his promises.

And that is why faith is so important. At the end of the
day, the Bible does not lie on the shelf like a passive object for
us to investigate. At the end of the day, it turns and looks at
us and asks, will you believe and trust? Or, as Lady Wisdom

[1]C. S. Lewis, *The Last Battle* (New York: Collier, 1956), 183.

cries out in the book of Proverbs, "Who will trust? Who will follow? Who will believe what I say?"

God gives his Word and his promises to us. He calls us to trust his Word and to believe his promises. Adam and Eve did not believe in the garden of Eden. Jesus believed throughout his life, and particularly in the garden of Gethsemane. And as you and I hear and believe God's Word, we are restored to the relationship with him for which we were made. This is the hope in which we can trust, because this hope will not disappoint. This is what the Bible—Old Testament and New—is all about.

QUESTIONS FOR REFLECTION ON THE NEW TESTAMENT

1. Have you ever been given or achieved something you had sought for a long time, only to find yourself disappointed? When? Why were you disappointed? Is there anything in this world worth desiring that is not that way?

2. What is the main argument of the four Gospels?

3. What does *Christ* mean? What does *Messiah* mean?

4. Explain the riddle of the Old Testament. Explain how Christ alone solves that riddle.

5. As we have seen, Jesus, the Lion of the tribe of Judah, came to devour the enemy, sin. How was this lion able to devour this enemy?

6. What do the New Testament Epistles, generally speaking, attempt to accomplish?

7. What does it mean to refer to Christ as our "priest"? How does he act as our priest?

8. As we have seen, Christians are counted as perfectly righteous today, even though we are by no means perfect. Is this a contradiction? How does this work?

9. Earlier, we considered the kind of people who try to protect their hearts by hoping only for things that they have

the power to control or make happen. Then we saw that Christianity calls for the exact opposite. How? Why?

10. Why is it significant that the heavenly city is shaped like a cube?

11. As we have considered, some of the very things you hope for right now are what God in his great love wants to pry from your fingers so that you can receive what is better from him. What might he want to pry from your fingers? What dream, hope, ambition, demand, expectation, possession, or person are you tightly clutching that he might ask you to surrender?

12. Surrendering the things we long for requires a kind of death—the death of a desire. And willfully choosing that death is hard to do. It requires us to believe—really believe!—that what God promises is even better. Can you remember a time in your life when God proved himself faithful to his promise of something better? Do you think he would do otherwise next time?

13. The end of Lewis's *The Last Battle* is marvelous, isn't it? A stanza in John Newton's hymn "Amazing Grace" evokes a similar sentiment when it begins, "When we've been there ten thousand years, bright shining as the sun . . ." Take a few moments to consider: what will all the things that have seemed so important to you over this last week look like in ten thousand years? Ten thousand years from now, what do you think you will want to have done this coming week?

14. In sixty seconds or less, explain the good news of Christianity.

SUBJECT INDEX

SCRIPTURE INDEX

9Marks

Building Healthy Churches

9Marks exists to equip church leaders with a biblical vision and practical resources for displaying God's glory to the nations through healthy churches.

To that end, we want to see churches characterized by these nine marks of health:

1 Expositional Preaching
2 Biblical Theology
3 A Biblical Understanding of the Gospel
4 A Biblical Understanding of Conversion
5 A Biblical Understanding of Evangelism
6 Biblical Church Membership
7 Biblical Church Discipline
8 Biblical Discipleship
9 Biblical Church Leadership

Find all our Crossway titles
and other resources at
www.9Marks.org